FOREWORD

　本書は現代の多様な位相を概観できる 5 つのテーマを選び、世界のさまざまな
地域の事情をさまざまな切り口で探っていくリーディング教材です。

　「芸術」「言語」「食育」「働き方改革」「歴史遺産」という 5 つのテーマは一見
繋がりがないかもしれません。しかし、この教科書のねらいは一つの事象につい
て専門的に系統だって知識を深める〔　　　　　　　　　　〕めて知る多
種多様な事象やユニークなものの見〔　　　　　　　　　　〕意見を持つ
のか考えたり、自分なりの興味関心に〔　　　　　　　　　　〕チャプター
同士を結びつけたりすることにより、〔　　　　　　　　　　〕ります。

　一冊読み終える頃には、知的な回路が増強され、しなやかな思考力が養われて
いるのではないかと期待しています。

　練習問題は下記の 3 つに目標を定めて作成されています。

(1) 文脈から言葉の意味を考えることによって、ボキャブラリーの増補と読解
　　力の向上を同時に達成する

(2) True or False や選択問題を通して、文意を大まかに掴むクセをつけ、同時
　　に必要なディテールを押さえる

(3) アクティブ・ラーニングの課題を通して、他者の意見を踏まえて自分なり
　　の考えを深め、発信する訓練をする

　英語を通して世界のさまざまな社会問題——すべて皆さんの身近で起きている
こと——を是非知ってください。

編著者

　2019 年秋

CONTENTS

1 》 ART 芸術

Chapter 1 ▶ 4
What's the Difference Between Modern
and Contemporary Art?

Chapter 2 ▶ 10
Jeff Koons And His Balloon Dogs

Chapter 3 ▶ 16
The Contemporaries: Mary Sibande

2 》 LANGUAGE 言語

Chapter 4 ▶ 22
What Languages Are Spoken in the Philippines?

Chapter 5 ▶ 28
'Latinx' Explained: A History of
the Controversial Word and How to Pronounce It

Chapter 6 ▶ 34
English Is the Language of Science.
That Isn't Always a Good Thing

3 》 FOOD EDUCATION 食育

Chapter 7 ▶ 40
School Feeding Schemes Can Fill
Children's Tummies and Farmers' Pockets

Chapter 8 ▶ 46
If You're Poor in America,
You Can Be Both Overweight and Hungry

Chapter 9 ▶ 52
This Supermarket Sells Only Wasted Food

4 ≫ WORK STYLE 働き方改革

Chapter 10 ▶ **58**
The Missing Women in Workforce Data

Chapter 11 ▶ **64**
Saudi Women Join the Workforce
as Country Reforms

Chapter 12 ▶ **70**
Migrant Workers in Thailand Live Harsh,
But Improving, Reality

5 ≫ HERITAGE 歴史遺産

Chapter 13 ▶ **76**
A Modern History of the Ogasawara Islands:
Migration, Diversity, and War

Chapter 14 ▶ **82**
Reggae Officially Declared
Global Cultural Treasure

Chapter 15 ▶ **88**
Chernobyl and the Dangerous Ground
of 'Dark Tourism'

Chapter 1 | What's the Difference Between Modern and Contemporary Art?

Modern art も contemporary art も日本語にするとどちらも「現代アート」であるが、その二つは違うものである。現代アートと現代アートの違いを探ってみよう。

>> Pre-reading Vocabulary Check

日本語の意味に合う英文になるよう適切なものを選びなさい。必要に応じて形を変えなさい。

・term　・shift　・phase　・surface　・notion

1. その芸術家の技は表面から見えないところにある。

The artist's art lies beneath the _____.

2. 製造業からサービス産業への大きな転換があった。

There was a major _____ from manufacturing to service industries.

3. 辞めようなんて考えは馬鹿げている。

The _____ of resigning is absurd.

4. 「自撮り」という語は 2000 年代に作られた。

The _____ "selfie" was coined in the 2000s.

5. 歴史の新しい段階に入った。

We have entered a new _____ in history.

>> Reading Passage

🔊 Audio 02

1 Have you ever wondered about the difference between modern and contemporary art? Well, first of all, the two terms are not interchangeable. There is a difference, and it is based on rough date ranges established by

© Todamo / Shutterstock.com Donald Judd, untitled (1973) artwork of plywood parallelepiped structures in the National Art Gallery in Ottawa

art historians, art critics, curators, art institutions, and the like, who recognized a distinct shift that took place, marking the end of Modernism 5 and the beginning of the contemporary age. Modern art is that which was created sometime between the 1860s and the late 1960s. Art made thereafter (e.g., conceptual, minimalist,* postmodern, feminist*) is considered contemporary.

"The Railway" by Édouard Manet © 1873

2 Beyond the time frames, 10 there are conceptual and aesthetic differences between the two phases. Art was called "modern" because it did not build on what came before 15 it or rely on the teachings of the art academies. Many art historians consider Édouard Manet to have been the first modern artist not only because he was depicting scenes of modern life but 20 also because he broke with tradition when he made no attempt to mimic the real world by way of perspective* tricks. He, instead, drew attention to the fact that his work of art was simply paint on a flat canvas and that it was made by using a paint brush, a paint brush that sometimes left its mark on the surface of the composition. While this shocked audiences 25 and critics, it inspired his peers and the next several generations of artists, each of which, whether in abstract works or representational, experimented with how to draw more attention to their medium.

Modern art encompasses numerous movements: Impressionism, Cubism, Surrealism, and Abstract Expressionism,* to name just a few.*

3 Contemporary art means art of the moment, but defining it beyond that and its open-ended date range is challenging, as the very notion of defining art became a personal quest in the hands of each artist, which resulted in ever-expanding possibilities. A key distinction between modern and contemporary art was a shift in focus away from aesthetic beauty to the underlying concept of the work (conceptual art and performance art are good examples). The end result of a work of contemporary art became less important than the process by which the artist arrived there, a process that now sometimes required participation on the part of the audience. So, the next time you are at a cocktail party and someone starts talking about modern art, you'll know not to pipe up about your favorite Jeff Koons inflated dog sculpture.*

NOTES

* **minimalist** : ここでは minimalism（ミニマリズム）あるいは minimal art（ミニマル・アート）を指し、1960 年代に音楽・美術の分野で生まれた装飾を必要最小限まで省いた表現スタイルのことを指す。

* **feminist** : ここでは feminist art（フェミニズム・アート）あるいは feminist art（フェミニスト・アート）を指す。

* **perspective** : 遠近法

* **Cubism, Surrealism, and Abstract Expressionism** : キュビズム、シュールレアリスム、抽象表現主義（いずれもモダニズムの美術様式）。

* **to name just a few** :（文末で）「これらはほんのわずかな例にすぎない」の意味。

* **So, the next time... Jeff Koons inflated dog sculpture.** : ジェフ・クーンズの彫刻が「モダン・アート」ではなく、「コンテンポラリー・アート」であることをここでは言っているのだが、その理由を Chapter 2 で考えてみよう。

» Post-reading Vocabulary Check

➤ 日本語の意味に合う英文になるよう、次の中から適切な 動詞 を選び、必要に応じて形を変えなさい。

・range　　・mark　　・rely　　・mimic　　・inspire　　・encompass

1. 価格は 1 億円から 10 億円まである。

The prices _____ from 100 million yen to 1 billion yen.

2. その石碑は古戦場跡を示す。

The stone _____ the site of the old battle field.

3. 彼の議論は問題のすべてを網羅している。

His argument _____ all the subjects.

4. その猿は人の仕草を真似ることができる。

This monkey can _____ a person's gesture.

5. 彼女をあてにすることができます。

You can _____ on her.

6. 詩神がシェイクスピアにひらめきを与えた。

The muse _____ Shakespeare.

➤ 下記の 形容詞または副詞 ＝英英・英日の語義が成立するように、空欄を埋めなさい。太字の形容詞または副詞が空欄の場合は本文中から適切な単語を探して埋めましょう。

1. d ☐☐☐☐☐☐☐ = recognizably different from something「はっきりした」

2. t ☐☐☐☐☐☐☐☐ = following that「それ以降」

3. a ☐☐☐☐☐☐☐ = relating to the beautiful「美的な」

4. a ☐☐☐☐☐☐ = intellectual, theoretical「抽象的な」

5. r ☐☐☐☐☐☐☐☐☐☐☐☐ = trying to show things as they really are
「具象的な」

6. numerous = m ☐☐☐「多数の」

7. challenging = difficult, t ☐☐☐☐「難易度が高い」

>> Comprehension Check True or False

下の英文が本文の内容として正しい場合は T、間違っている場合は F を選びましょう。

1. Modern art and contemporary art are interchangeable. (T / F)

2. Édouard Manet is a contemporary artist. (T / F)

3. Contemporary art puts an emphasis more on the concept of work than aesthetic beauty. (T / F)

>> ACTIVE LEARNING for Keyword Check

本文に出てくる重要な単語についてペアまたはグループになって調べて表を完成させなさい。

用　語	概　要
Modernism モダニズム／モダニズム芸術	
postmodernism (postmodern) ポスト・モダニズム／ ポスト・モダン芸術	主に 1980 年代に席巻した思想的潮流を指すが、特定の主義や様式を指すものではない。ひとまず共通点として、モダニズムに反発し、それを越えようとした芸術様式とまとめることができる。典型的には、異質な要素を折衷したり、過去の作品を引用したりする特徴がある。
Édouard Manet エドゥアール・マネ	
Impressionism 印象主義	

>> Comprehension Check Multiple Choice

本文の内容に照らして最も正しいものを a ～ c の中から選んで○をつけなさい。

1. Modern art was active:

  a. between the 1860s and the 1960s

  b. before the late 1860s

  c. after the 1960s

2. Which of the following belongs to contemporary art?

  a. Surrealism

  b. feminism art

  c. Impressionism

3. Which is the most important element of contemporary art?

  a. the teachings of the art academies

  b. perspective

  c. processes

>> English Composition for Idiom Learning

📶 Audio 03

日本語の意味に合うよう、（　　　）内を並べ替えて英文を完成させましょう。並べ替え部分には本文中に登場するイディオムが含まれています。なお、文頭に来る語も小文字にしてあります。

1. 事故は 3 時から 4 時までの間に起こった。

(took, between, accident, place, the, 3 and 4 o'clock).

_____

2. 彼は頑張って眠ろうとしたが、だめだった。

(attempt, sleep, he, an, to, made), but failed.

_____

3. 彼女の仕事は大儲けの結果となった。

(has, her, resulted, profit, a, work, in, large,).

_____

Chapter 2 | Jeff Koons And His Balloon Dogs

これまでに4度盗作疑惑で訴訟を起こされ有罪判決を受けている、アメリカの現代アート界に物議をかもすジェフ・クーンズとはどんな人物で、彼の彫刻作品群「バルーン・ドッグ」とはどんな作品なのでしょう。

» Pre-reading Vocabulary Check

日本語の意味に合う英文になるよう適切なものを選びなさい。必要に応じて形を変えなさい。

- obsession　・concern　・controversial　・commerce　・actual

1. それは非常に物議をかもす新計画だ。

It is the highly _____ new plan.

2. その見積もりは実際のコストよりもはるかに少額だった。

The estimate was much less than the _____ cost.

3. その問題は私たち全員にとって関心事であるはずだ。

The issue should be of _____ to us all.

4. 税率の変更はビジネスに有益である。

The changes in taxation are of benefit to _____.

5. 彼女は潔癖さに強迫観念がある。

She has an _____ with cleanliness.

» Reading Passage

🔊 Audio 04

1 On this day in 1955 one of the most controversial artists of the 20th century was born. Jeff Koons is the artist who blended the concerns and methods of Pop, Conceptual, and appropriation art with craft-making and

© Hayk_Shalunts / Shutterstock.com *Balloon Dog* by Jeff Koons at The Broad Contemporary Art Museum

popular culture to create his own unique iconography,* often controversial and always engaging. His work explores contemporary obsessions with sex and desire; race and gender; and celebrity, media, commerce, and fame. A self-proclaimed* "idea man," Koons hires artisans and technicians to make the actual works.

2 His works have sold for substantial sums, including at least one world record auction price for a work by a living artist. On November 12, 2013, Koons's Balloon Dog (Orange) sold at Christie's* Post-War and Contemporary Art Evening Sale in New York City for US$58.4 million, above its high US$55 million estimate, becoming the most expensive work by a living artist sold at auction.

3 The stainless steel orange sculpture with transparent color coating is one of the first balloon dogs, which look like the kind of souvenir clowns make at birthday parties. Other pups have been on display around the world in red, green, and blue – not to mention a shiny pink one made it to Versailles in 2008.

4 Koons said, "I've always enjoyed balloon animals because they're like us. We're balloons. You take a breath and you inhale, it's an optimism. You exhale, and it's kind of a symbol of death."

© Hayk_Shalunts / Shutterstock.com *Balloon Monkey* by Jeff Koons at Los Angeles County Museum

5 The Balloon Dog is not the only Balloon sculptures of Koons – below is a glimpse at other noteworthy balloon sculptures by Koons in recent years:

25

6 The shocking pink Balloon Dog exhibited at the Château de Versailles in 2008 sparked controversy as some visitors said the work was crude and too modern for Louis XIV's former palace.

7 The Balloon Dog also becomes a symbol of pop culture. Jay Z* apparently is a huge fan of Koons, once rapping "Oh what a feeling, f*** * it I want a billion / Jeff Koons balloons, I just wanna blow up" on his 2013 song "Picasso Baby." He also performed with a copy of it on his concerts in 2017.

30

NOTES

* iconography : 図象^{イコン}
* self-proclaimed : 自称
* Christie's : クリスティーズ（イギリス大手オークション会社）
* Jay Z : ジェイ・Z（1962- ）アメリカ合衆国のラッパーで起業家
* f*** : ひわいな言葉なので、スペルアウトすることを自粛して、続く三文字を *** で消している。

» Post-reading Vocabulary Check

➤ 日本語の意味に合う英文になるよう、次の中から適切な 動詞 を選び、必要に応じて形を変えなさい。

- blend　　・explore　　・spark　　・exhibit　　・hire　　・perform

1. 山登りに興味を持ったきっかけは何でしたか?

What was it that ＿＿＿＿＿ your interest in mountain climbing?

2. 古さと現代性がここでは見事に融合している。

Antiquity and modernity are happily ＿＿＿＿＿ together here.

3. 彼はある着想をさらに深く考えてみている。

He is ＿＿＿＿＿ an idea further.

4. エミリーはその会社の本社で雇われるだろう。

Emily will be ＿＿＿＿＿ at the head office of the company.

5. ダ・ヴィンチのモナリザはパリのルーヴル美術館に展示されている。

Da Vinci's Mona Lisa is ＿＿＿＿＿ at the Louvre Museum in Paris.

6. 彼女のバッハの作品の巧みな演奏ぶりに驚いた。

I was amazed at how well she ＿＿＿＿＿ the Bach piece.

➤ 下記の 形容詞または副詞 ＝英英・英日の語義が成立するように、空欄を埋めなさい。太字の形容詞または副詞が空欄の場合は本文中から適切な単語を探して埋めましょう。

1. s □□□□□□□□□ = large in amount「相当な」

2. engaging = charming, a □□□□□□□□□「人を惹きつける」

3. living = a □□□□ now「現在生きている」

4. transparent = c □□□□「透明な」

5. noteworthy = worth paying a □□□□□□□ to「注目に値する」

6. c □□□□ = vulgar「下品な、洗練されていない」

7. f □□□□□ = last「旧〜」

8. a □□□□□□□□□ = as far as one knows or can see「見たところ〜らしい」

>> Comprehension Check `True or False`

下の英文が本文の内容として正しい場合は T、間違っている場合は F を選びましょう。

1. Koons makes his works by himself. （ T / F ）

2. One of Koon's Balloon Dogs sold for about $60 million. （ T / F ）

3. Jay-Z is a fan of Jeff Koons. （ T / F ）

>> ACTIVE LEARNING for Keyword Check

本文に出てくる重要な単語についてペアまたはグループになって調べて表を完成させなさい。

用　語	概　要	代表的なアーティスト・作品例
craft-making 手仕事／工芸	職人による高度な熟練技術によって作られた美的かつ実用的なもの、およびそれを製作する分野のこと。用途は生活の隅々に及び、材料も多岐に渡る。	
pop art ポップ・アート		アンディ・ウォーホル「キャンベルスープの缶」
conceptual art コンセプチュアル・アート／概念芸術		マルセル・デュシャン「泉」（先駆的な存在） ジョセフ・コスース「1つおよび3つの椅子」
appropriation art アプロプリエーション・アート／盗用芸術		村上隆「DOB」 ジェフ・クーンズ「バルーン・ドッグ」

≫ Comprehension Check **Multiple Choice**

本文の内容に照らして最も正しいものを a 〜 c の中から選んで○をつけなさい。

1. Which of the following does Koons's work explore?

    a. contemporary obsessions with sex and desire

    b. money

    c. aesthetic beauty

2. Which of the following did Koons say was "a symbol of death"?

    a. to take a breath

    b. to exhale

    c. to inhale

3. Some visitors thought the shocking pink Balloon Dog was:

    a. not good

    b. fair

    c. admirable

≫ English Composition for Idiom Learning

🔊 Audio 05

日本語の意味に合うよう、（　　　）内を並べ替えて英文を完成させましょう。並べ替え部分には本文中に登場するイディオムが含まれています。なお、文頭に来る語も小文字にしてあります。

1. 彼の作品は市立博物館に展示されている。

  (are, display, works, museum, city, his, the, at, on).

  _____

2. 車庫がないのはもちろん、うちでは車を買う余裕がない。

  We can't afford a car, (mention, the, have, fact, not, that, we, to, garage, no).

  _____

3. そのチームは準々決勝へ進出するだろう。

  (it, team, quarterfinals, make, will, to, the, the).

  _____

Chapter 3 | The Contemporaries: Mary Sibande

南アフリカのヨハネスブルグを拠点とする彫刻家のメアリー・シバンドの青いメイド服の彫刻のモチーフはどこから借用され、どのようなコンセプトがこめられているのか、南アフリカの辿った歴史と併せて探ってみよう。

>> Pre-reading Vocabulary Check

日本語の意味に合う英文になるよう適切なものを選びなさい。必要に応じて形を変えなさい。

> · era   · margin   · narrative   · celebrate   · oppression

1. ビクトリア朝時代ではそのような行為は受け入れられなかった。

In the Victorian _____ such behavior was unacceptable.

2. 詩人は田園のすばらしさをほめたたえた。

The poet _____ the glory of the countryside.

3. 彼の話は個人的体験に基づくものであった。

His _____ was based on his personal experiences.

4. 彼らは社会の端で暮らしている。

They live on the _____ of society.

5. 彼らは国を圧政から救うために戦った。

They fought to free their country from _____.

>> Reading Passage

🔊 Audio 06

1 Mary Sibande – a sculptor, photographer, and visual artist based in Johannesburg – is interested primarily in questions of the body and how to reclaim* the black female body in post-colonial* and post-apartheid*

They Don't Make Them Like They Used To. © lev radin / Shutterstock.com, New York, Visitors attend Armory Show Gallery MOMO presentation work by artist Mary Sibande at Piers 92 & 94

South Africa.

2 She often works through an alter-ego, Sophie, a sculptural figure who ₅
traverses the uncanny valleys* of liminal space. Sophie is personal. Her
visage is modeled largely after the artist herself, and she draws on* the
history of the women in Sibande's family who worked as maids
throughout the apartheid and post-apartheid eras. But Sophie is also
symbolic, a figure that stands in to speak for femininity, blackness, ₁₀
labour, post-coloniality, and communities on the margin as a whole. She
moves in between history and contemporary life. Sophie bears the weight
of centuries-old colonial narratives attempting to make the African
woman invisible. At the same time, Sophie's dress, the familiar bright
blue of contemporary domestic* uniforms, reminds us of the kinds of ₁₅
subjugation* that lingers* in our society.

3 Sophie is both real and surreal: her calm disposition is juxtaposed with
overflowing, colorful Victorian* garb (*I'm a Lady*, 2010), or she is dressed
in traditional maid attire, stitching the hem of a Superman cape (*They
Don't Make Them Like They Used To,* 2008). Sophie is both active and ₂₀
passive: the static sculpture, eyes closed, is but* still in a moment of glory,
wielding a larger-than-life cavalry mare* (*The Reign,* 2010) or singing to a

great, anonymous orchestra (*Silent Symphony,* 2010).

4 For all the histories of oppression Sibande's alter-ego seeks to critique,
she transcends above them, reclaiming her space as a subject in both
historical and contemporary narratives. Ultimately, Sophie is a
celebration. Sibande says, "My work is not about complaining about
Apartheid, or an invitation to feel sorry for me because I am black and my
mothers were maids. It is about celebrating what we are as women in
South Africa today. We need to go back to see what we are celebrating. To
celebrate, I needed to bring this maid."

5 Largely, Sibande's work draws inspiration from her individual
experience growing up in South Africa. The artist's focus on "the maid" is
often cited as homage to her family, of which four generations of women
served as domestic workers. Sibande has often attributed her fascination
with fashion and fabric as performance to a lifelong fascination with the
"Sunday special clothes*" community members wore to church.

NOTES

* **reclaim**：再生する
* **post-colonial**：植民地独立後の、ポスト・コロニアルの
* **post-apartheid**：アパルトヘイト撤廃後の
* **uncanny valleys**：不気味の谷（《現象》人間の似姿をした人工的創作物が人間に近づきある領域
   にいくと、似ていると感心するよりも不気味さや嫌悪感を覚える現象）
* **draw on**：（素材として）利用する
* **domestic**：（名）メイド（domestic worker も同じ）
* **subjugation**：服従させること
* **linger**：残存する
* **Victorian**：（重厚で装飾に凝っている）ビクトリア朝風の
* **but**：本当に、ただただ（quite）
* **cavalry mare**：騎馬
* **Sunday special clothes**：よそゆきの服

≫ Post-reading Vocabulary Check

➤ 日本語の意味に合う英文になるよう、次の中から適切な 動詞 を選び、必要に応じて形を変えなさい。

・cite　・traverse　・juxtapose　・seek　・transcend　・serve

1. 彼女はホイットマンの詩をスピーチで引用した。

She _____ Whitman's poem in her speech.

2. 鉄道の線路がこの地点で道を横断している。

The railway tracks _____ the road at this point.

3. 彼の居間はアンティーク家具とモダンな家具が並置されている。

His living room _____ antiques with modern furniture.

4. 神は人知を超越している。

God _____ all human knowledge.

5. 彼らは海の環境を改善しようと努めた。

They _____ to improve the environment in the ocean.

6. 彼女は 20 年間、市長を務めた。

She _____ as mayor for twenty years.

➤ 下記の 形容詞または副詞 ＝英英・英日の語義が成立するように、空欄を埋めなさい。太字の形容詞または副詞が空欄の場合は本文中から適切な単語を探して埋めましょう。

1. primarily = m □□□□□ 「主として」

2. l □□□□□□ = in-between, transitional 「境界線上の」

3. p □□□□□□□ = in person and in the flesh 「人格がある、血肉の通った」

4. s □□□□□□ = strange 「現実離れした」

5. s □□□□□ = fixed, unchanged, still 「静止した」

6. a □□□□□□□□ = unknown, unnamed 「無名の」

7. u □□□□□□□□□ = fundamentally, essentially 「究極的に」

>> Comprehension Check `True or False`

下の英文が本文の内容として正しい場合は T、間違っている場合は F を選びましょう。

1. Sophie's visage is based on Sibande's mother.   (T / F)

2. Sophie has opposite personalities at the same time.   (T / F)

3. Sibande has been fascinated with "Sunday special clothes."   (T / F)

>> ACTIVE LEARNING for Keyword Check & Discussion

➤ 本文に出てくる重要な単語についてペアまたはグループになって調べて表を完成させなさい。

用　語	概　要
apartheid アパルトヘイト	

➤ p. 17 の写真のシバンドの作品 *They Don't Make Them Like They Used To.* を見て、そのコンセプトや感想をペアまたはグループで話し合ってみましょう。

_____

_____

_____

_____

_____

>> Comprehension Check `Multiple Choice`

本文の内容に照らして最も正しいものを a 〜 c の中から選んで○をつけなさい。

1. Which of the following does Sibande try to reclaim?

   a. South Africa

   b. the black female body

   c. her family

2. Which of the following does Sophie's blue dress remind us of?

   a. Victorian era

   b. femininity

   c. subjugation

3. Which of the following is Sibande's ultimate purpose in her work?

   a. celebration

   b. complaining about Apartheid

   c. criticizing the histories of oppression

>> English Composition for Idiom Learning   🔊 Audio 07

日本語の意味に合うよう、（　　　）内を並べ替えて英文を完成させましょう。並べ替え部分には本文中に登場するイディオムが含まれています。なお、文頭に来る語も小文字にしてあります。

1. 展覧会は概して良くなかったが、彼女の彫刻は鑑賞する価値があった。

(exhibition, as, so, the, was, a, not, whole) good, but her sculptures were worth seeing.

---

2. 政治活動を色々としているが、彼は本質的には学者だ。

(for, political, all, activities, his), he is a scholar in essence.

---

3. 彼らは彼女の成功を勤勉のおかげだとしている。

(her, they, success, attribute, to, work, hard).

Chapter 4

What Languages Are Spoken in the Philippines?

公用語や国語が何であるか意識したことはあるだろうか。言語的に複雑な歴史を持ち、かつ多言語が話されるフィリピンのような国ではどのようになっているのか言語事情を探ってみよう。

≫ Pre-reading Vocabulary Check

日本語の意味に合う英文になるよう適切なものを選びなさい。必要に応じて形を変えなさい。

・rule　・occupation　・constitution　・congress　・exception

1. 憲法は国の基本的な方針であり法律である。

A _____ is the basic principles and laws of a nation.

2. スペインはその地域を占領していた。

Spain was in _____ of the region.

3. 議会は教育予算の支出を認めた。

_____ approved funds for education.

4. どの法則にも例外がある。

Every rule has its _____.

5. 彼は植民地支配下にあった国を解放した。

He released the country under colonial _____.

≫ Reading Passage

 Audio 08

1 Official Languages Spoken in the Philippines

During colonial rule, the official language of the Philippines was Spanish. Even after the territory was ceded to the US at the end of the 19th

century, Spanish remained the lingua franca for another century or so. In 1901, under US occupation, English became the language of the public 5 school system. The Constitution of 1935 established both English and Spanish as the official languages of the country with a note that Congress should nominate a native language with national standing*. The Congress voted to include Tagalog as the national language in 1937.

2 Tagalog became known as Pilipino in 1959. The Constitution was again amended in 1973, naming Pilipino and English as the official languages of the country. At this time, Congress decided that a new national language, called Filipino, should be developed. When the Constitution was again amended in 1987, Filipino and  10

15

English became the co-official languages. English is primarily used in printed publications, such as newspapers and magazines. 20

3 **National Language of the Philippines**

In addition to being one of the official languages of the country, Filipino is also the national language. This language primarily consists of Tagalog with some mix of other Philippine languages. Public school teachers rely on Filipino to teach most classes, and it is the language of choice* for 25 televised media and cinema. Today, it has become the lingua franca throughout the majority of the country as well as in Philippine communities around the world.

4 Regional Languages of the Philippines

Twenty-one languages are spoken regionally. Each of these represents a major indigenous language of the Philippines that is spoken in areas inhabited by large populations of native speakers. The majority of these regional languages belong to the Malayo-Polynesian language family* sub-group, and this sub-group belongs to the Austronesian language family*. This is true with the exception of Chavacano, which is a Spanish-based creole language. It is the only Spanish-based Creole language in Asia and has been spoken for around 400 years. This makes the language one of the oldest Creole languages in the world. Chavacano has an estimated 1.2 million speakers.

5 Foreign Languages Spoken in the Philippines

Not all of the languages spoken in the Philippines are indigenous. This country is home to a large number of immigrants as well, which is reflected in its wide variety of foreign languages. Many regional languages here have borrowed loanwords from several of these languages, particularly for food and household items.

NOTES

* **The Constitution of 1935...national standing.**：1935年 憲法第8条3項 は、「フィリピン議会は既存のフィリピン諸語の一つに基づいて共通の国語を開発し採用するための措置を講ずること。法律で制定されるまでは、英語とスペイン語を公用語とする」ことを定めた。(内山史子「フィリピンの国民形成についての一考察―― 1934年 憲法制定議会 における国語制定議論」『東南アジア――歴史と文化』29号、2000年、91頁)
* **of choice**：一般に好まれる
* **Malayo-Polynesian language family**：マレー・ポリネシア語族
* **Austronesian language family**：オーストロネシア語族

≫ Post-reading Vocabulary Check

➤ 日本語の意味に合う英文になるよう、次の中から適切な 動詞 を選び、必要に応じて形を変えなさい。

> ・nominate　・vote　・amend　・consist　・inhabit　・reflect

1. このアパートには 100 世帯以上が住んでいる。

The apartments are _____ by more than 100 families.

2. その小説はヴィクトリア朝時代のモラルや習慣を反映している。

The novel _____ the morals and customs of the Victorian era.

3. 1937 年、フィリピンの女性は選挙権を獲得した。

In 1937 Filipino women got the right to _____.

4. ウォルト・ホイットマンの『草の葉』は 389 編の詩から成っている。

Walt Whitman's *Leaves of Grass* _____ of 389 poems.

5. 汝の道と行ないを正せ。

_____ your ways and your doings.

6. 彼女の最新の映画はアカデミー賞の候補になった。

Her latest film was _____ for an Academy Award.

➤ 下記の 形容詞または副詞 =英英・英日の語義が成立するように、空欄を埋めなさい。太字の形容詞または副詞が空欄の場合は本文中から適切な単語を探して埋めましょう。

1. o □□□□□□□ = authorized, formal「公的な」

2. n □□□□□□□ = public, governmental「国家の、全国的な」

3. n □□□□□ = inborn, innate「土着の、生まれつきの」

4. regional = l □□□□「地方の、地域の」

5. i □□□□□□□□□ = occurring naturally in a particular region「土着の」

6. particularly = s □□□□□□□□□□□「特に」

7. household = d □□□□□□□「家庭の」

≫ Comprehension Check True or False

下の英文が本文の内容として正しい場合は T、間違っている場合は F を選びましょう。

1. Spanish is an official language in the Philippines.   (T / F)

2. Filipino is based on Tagalog.   (T / F)

3. Chavacano belongs to the Austronesian language family.   (T / F)

≫ ACTIVE LEARNING for Keyword Check

本文に出てくる重要な単語についてペアまたはグループになって調べて表を完成させなさい。

用　語・テーマ	概　要
The differences between an official language and a national language 公用語と国語の違い	
lingua franca リンガ・フランカ	
creole language クレオール語	

≫ Comprehension Check **Multiple Choice**

本文の内容に照らして最も正しいものをa～cの中から選んで○をつけなさい。

1. Which of the following is the correct combination of the official languages in the Philippines?

   a. English and Spanish

   b. English and Filipino

   c. Tagalog and Chavacano

2. How many major indigenous languages in the Philippines are there?

   a. 21

   b. 400

   c. 1.2 million

3. In the Philippines, loanwords are often used as words related to:

   a. school

   b. televised media

   c. food

≫ English Composition for Idiom Learning

🔊 Audio 09

日本語の意味に合うよう、（　　）内を並べ替えて英文を完成させましょう。並べ替え部分には本文中に登場するイディオムが含まれています。なお、文頭に来る語も小文字にしてあります。

1. 偉大な政治家だったことに加えて、彼は学者としても一流だった。

(great, a, addition, being, in, politician, to), (scholar, a, was, he, leading).

_____

2. 患者たちは新薬に頼っている。

(on, patients, drug, the, new, rely, the).

_____

3. 彼女はスペイン語だけでなくチャバカノ語も話せる。

(Chavacano, speak, she, as, can, as, well, Spanish).

_____

Chapter 5 | 'Latinx' Explained: A History of the Controversial Word and How to Pronounce It

従来の言語構造は男女の性差やその権力構造に基づいて成立しており、性的マイノリティの存在はないものとされていた。'Latinx' という言葉が浮き彫りにする、言語に内在するイデオロギーや歴史を探ろう。

≫ Pre-reading Vocabulary Check

日本語の意味に合う英文になるよう適切なものを選びなさい。必要に応じて形を変えなさい。

・descent　・advocate　・alternative　・masculine　・reject

1. 彼は代替エネルギー源開発の積極的な支持者である。

He is an active _____ of alternative energy sources.

2. ヨーロッパはそれが公平なものでない限り、アメリカの中東和平案を却下するだろう。

Europe will _____ any US Middle East peace plan unless it is fair.

3. 英語には男性名詞および女性名詞がない。

English has no _____ and feminine nouns.

4. スチュワーデスという言葉はジェンダーの区別がない代替案のフライト・アテンダントに置き換えられた。

The term stewardess was replaced by the gender-neutral _____ flight attendant.

5. 私はアイルランドとアフリカの血を受け継いでいる。

I am of Irish-African _____.

》Reading Passage

Audio 10

1 "Latinx" is a gender-neutral term used in lieu of "Latino" or "Latina" to refer to a person of Latin American descent.

2 Using the term "Latinx" to refer to all people of Latin American decent has become more common as members in the LGBTQ community and its advocates have embraced the label. The gendered structure of the 5 Spanish language has made "Latinx" both an inclusive and controversial term.

3 Pronounced "luh-TEE-neks," Merriam-Webster dictionary added the word in 2018 to describe those of Latin American descent who don't want to be identified by gender, or who don't identify as being male or female. 10

4 The word was created as a gender-neutral alternative to "Latinos," not only to better include those who are gender fluid, but also to push back on* the inherently masculine term used to describe all genders in the Spanish language.

5 Even though "Latinos" technically refers to all genders of Latin 15 American descent, it's still a masculine word in Spanish.

6 For example, a group of females would be called "Latinas" and a group of males would be called "Latinos." However, a group of males and females of Latin American descent would revert to the masculine "Latinos." 20

7 George Cadava, Director of the Latina and Latino Studies program at Northwestern University, said terms to describe Latin Americans in the U.S. have constantly been evolving over the course of history. "Latinos"

gained popularity as a rejection of the word "Hispanic," which many
argued was imposed by the government.

8 "Latinx is an even further evolution that was meant to be inclusive of people who are queer or lesbian or gay or transgender," said Cadava. "In some cases, it was a rejection of binary gender politics."

9 However, as "Latinx" grows in popularity, it also becomes more controversial within the Latin American community. The word was rejected in 2018 by the Real Academia Española,* the official source on the Spanish language. Many who agree with this decision believe it is important to conserve the language, which is spoken by over 500 million

people, according to a 2017 report by the Cervantes Institute* in Spain.

10 Another argument against "Latinx" is that it erases feminist movements in the 1970s that fought to represent women with the word "Latina," Cadava said.

NOTES

* push back on：却下する
* the Real Academia Española：スペイン国立言語アカデミー（スペイン語の標準を決定している機関）
* the Cervantes Institute：インスティトゥト・セルバンテス（1991 年、スペイン政府が設立したスペイン語教育およびスペイン語圏文化普及を目的とした機関）

≫ Post-reading Vocabulary Check

➤ 日本語の意味に合う英文になるよう、次の中から適切な 動詞 を選び、必要に応じて形を変えなさい。

- refer　・embrace　・identify　・evolve　・impose　・conserve

1. 政府は輸入車に関税を課している。

The government _____ a duty on imported cars.

2. 著者は自伝の中で一度彼に言及した。

The author _____ to him once in his autobiography.

3. 彼らはアマゾンの森林を守るのに尽力している。

They devote themselves to _____ the Amazon forest.

4. 母親は子供の決断を受け入れた。

The mother _____ her child's decision.

5. ロサンゼルス警察は遺体の身元を特定した。

The LAPD _____ the body.

6. 人類は霊長類の祖先から進化した。

The human species _____ from primate ancestors.

➤ 下記の 形容詞または副詞 ＝英英・英日の語義が成立するように、空欄を埋めなさい。太字の形容詞または副詞が空欄の場合は本文中から適切な単語を探して埋めましょう。

1. g □□□□□□□ = of specific to the male or female sex「性の区別がある」

2 i □□□□□□□□ = with everything included「すべてを含んだ」

3. i □□□□□□□□□ = essentially, basically「本質的に」

4. technically = s □□□□□□ speaking「厳密に言えば」

5. c □□□□□□□□□ = always, continually「絶えず」

6. b □□□□□ = consisting of two things or parts「二元 (論) の」

>> Comprehension Check ⟨True or False⟩

下の英文が本文の内容として正しい場合は T、間違っている場合は F を選びましょう。

1. Latinx doesn't identify one's gender.   (T / F)

2. Many people think that the word "Hispanic" was forced by the government.

(T / F)

3. All Latin American descents embrace the word 'Latinx.'   (T / F)

>> ACTIVE LEARNING for Keyword Check & Discussion

➤ 本文に出てくる重要な単語についてペアまたはグループになって調べて表を完成させなさい。

用　語	概　要
Hispanic ヒスパニック	
gender-fluid(ity) 性差流動性／ ジェンダー・フルイディティ	

➤ 伝統的な言語構造や言語成立の歴史を遺産として保持していくべきか、時代や価値観の変遷によって言語も変えていくべきか、それぞれの例を出し、ペアまたはグループで考えを話し合ってみましょう。

_____

_____

_____

» Comprehension Check Multiple Choice

本文の内容に照らして最も正しいものを a ～ c の中から選んで○をつけなさい。

1. Which of the following terms do LGBTQ community members embrace?

  a. Latina

  b. Hispanic

  c. Latinx

2. Which of the following is "a feminine term"?

  a. Latina

  b. Hispanic

  c. Latinx

3. Which of the following does NOT apply to what those who reject the term "Latinx" see important?

  a. the conservation of Spanish language

  b. the history of the word "Latina"

  c. the rejection of gender politics

» English Composition for Idiom Learning   Audio 11

日本語の意味に合うよう、（　　　）内を並べ替えて英文を完成させましょう。並べ替え部分には本文中に登場するイディオムが含まれています。なお、文頭に来る語も小文字にしてあります。

1. たとえ彼女が反対しても私は賛成する。

  (she, agree, even, I'll, though, disagrees).

_____

2. 私はこの詩が何を言わんとしているのかわからない。

  (this, can't, make, I, what, out, poem, is, to, say, meant).

_____

3. 破傷風は死に至る場合もある。

  (some, fatal, tetanus, is, in, cases).

_____

Chapter 6 English Is the Language of Science. That Isn't Always a Good Thing

>> Pre-reading Vocabulary Check

日本語の意味に合う英文になるよう適切なものを選びなさい。必要に応じて形を変えなさい。

> · breakthrough　· bias　· consequences　· assessment　· abstract

1. ペニシリンは革命的な大発見だった。

Penicillin was a revolutionary _____.

2. 150 語以内で論文の要約をしてください。

Please write an _____ of your paper within 150 words.

3. 女性のドライバーに偏見を抱いている人もいる。

Some have a _____ against female drivers.

4. 彼女の評価はいつも正しい。

She is always correct in her _____.

5. 彼女の決断は重大な結果をもたらすだろう。

Her decision will have grave _____.

科学分野の共通語が英語であることは周知のとおりであるが、このことが研究者間のコミュニケーションを容易にする一方、不都合や偏見を生み出してはいないだろうか。批判的な視点に立って考えてみよう。

》》 Reading Passage

🔊 Audio 12

1 A new study in the journal *PLOS Biology** sheds light on how widespread the gulf can be between English-language science and any-other-language science.

2 "Native English speakers tend to assume that all important information is in English," says Tatsuya Amano, a zoology researcher at the University of Cambridge and lead author* on this study. Amano, a native of Japan who has lived in Cambridge for five years, has encountered this bias in his own work as a zoologist; publishing in English was essential for him to further his career, he says. At the same time, he has seen studies that have been overlooked by global reviews, presumably because they were only published in Japanese.

3 Yet particularly when it comes to work about biodiversity* and conservation, Amano says, much of the most important data is collected and published by researchers in the countries where exotic or endangered species* live – not just the United States or England. This can lead to oversights of important statistics or critical breakthroughs by international organizations, or even scientists unnecessarily duplicating research that has already been done. Speaking for himself and his collaborators, he says: "We think ignoring non-English papers can cause biases in your understanding."

4 His study offers concrete examples of the consequences of science's English bias. For instance, the latest population data on the fairy pitta,* a bird species found in several Asian countries and classified as vulnerable,* was not included in the latest assessment by the International Union for the Conservation of Nature.* The reason, again, was that the paper was only published in Chinese.

5 Even for people who try not to ignore research published in non-English languages, Amano says, difficulties exist. More than half of the non-English papers observed in this study had no English title, abstract or keywords, making them all but* invisible to most scientists doing database searches in English. "I think this issue is actually much larger than many people think," Amano says.

6 Amano thinks that journals and scientific academies working to include international voices is one of the best solutions to this language gap. He suggests that all major efforts to compile reviews of research include speakers of a variety of languages so that important work isn't overlooked. He also suggests that journals and authors should be pushed to translate summaries of their work into several languages so that it's more easily found by people worldwide. Amano and his collaborators translated a summary of their work into Spanish, Chinese, Portuguese, French and Japanese.

NOTES

* *PLOS Biology*：『プロス・バイオロジー（生物学）』誌（アメリカの科学雑誌）
* **lead author**：筆頭著者
* **biodiversity**：生物多種多様性
* **exotic species**：外来種
* **endangered species**：絶滅危惧種
* **fairy pitta**：(鳥) ヤイロチョウ
* **vulnerable**：絶滅危惧Ⅱ類の
* **the International Union for the Conservation of Nature**：国際自然保護連合
* **all but**：ほとんど〜、〜も同然

» Post-reading Vocabulary Check

➤ 日本語の意味に合う英文になるよう、次の中から適切な 動詞 を選び、必要に応じて形を変えなさい。

> ・assume　・encounter　・duplicate　・classify　・suggest　・compile

1. これらの商品は大きさと色で分類されている。

These products have been _____ by size and color.

2. 彼は万が一の場合に備えていつも書類の写しを作る。

He always _____ documents just in case.

3. 女の子は森でばったりクマに遭遇した。

The girl _____ a bear in the woods.

4. 裁判官は彼女が正直だと思った。

The judge _____ that she was honest.

5. マーク・トウェインは自分の数々の旅行を本の形にまとめた。

Mark Twain _____ his travels in book form.

6. 彼の父は彼に留学を考えてみることを提案した。

His father _____ to him that he should consider studying abroad.

➤ 下記の 形容詞または副詞 ＝英英・英日の語義が成立するように、空欄を埋めなさい。太字の形容詞または副詞が空欄の場合は本文中から適切な単語を探して埋めましょう。

1. w □□□□□□□□□ = general, common「広がっている」

2. p □□□□□□□□ = all things considered, undoubtedly「（論理的に考えて）おそらく」

3. critical = i □□□□□□□□, crucial「重大な」

4. u □□□□□□□□□□□ = uselessly「不必要に」

5. c □□□□□□□ = solid, real「具体的な」

6. latest = most r □□□□□, newest「最新の」

7. i □□□□□□□□ = unnoticeable, unseen, hidden「人目につかない」

8. actually = in f □□□「実際には」

9. m □□□□ = main, outstanding「重要な」

》 Comprehension Check 　True or False

下の英文が本文の内容として正しい場合は T、間違っている場合は F を選びましょう。

1. Amano has no English papers. （ T / F ）

2. Oversights of non-English papers can cause scientists to duplicate research.

（ T / F ）

3. The latest population data on the fairy pitta is not important. （ T / F ）

》 ACTIVE LEARNING for Discussion

英語が世界の共通語となっているメリットとデメリットについて、（できれば、自分が学んだり興味を持っている分野［科目や専攻］に鑑みて）、ペアまたはグループで意見を出し話し合ってみましょう。

興味のある分野	メリット	デメリット

>> Comprehension Check Multiple Choice

本文の内容に照らして最も正しいものを a 〜 c の中から選んで○をつけなさい。

1. Which of the following tendencies applies to native English-speaking scientists?

   a. the tendency to fill the gulf between English-language science and any-other-language science

   b. the tendency to include the information of their work in several languages

   c. the tendency to assume that all critical information is in English

2. Which of the following is true about the reason why many non-English papers are overlooked?

   a. because they receive poor reviews

   b. because they have no information in English

   c. because they have their own academic communities

3. Which of the following does Amano ask scientists to do?

   a. to translate an abstract of their research into several languages

   b. to publish in English to further their career

   c. to make their work invisible to English-speaking scientists

>> English Composition for Idiom Learning

🔊 Audio 13

日本語の意味に合うよう、（　　　）内を並べ替えて英文を完成させましょう。並べ替え部分には本文中に登場するイディオムが含まれています。なお、文頭に来る語も小文字にしてあります。

1. そのことはまたアルツハイマー病の解明に光を投げかけている。

   (Alzheimer's, it, also, light, sheds, on, disease).

_____

2. 彼女は車のこととなると、お金を惜しまない。

   She (comes, extravagant, when, is, it, cars, to).

_____

3. 彼は成功できるように一生懸命働いている。

   (hard, he, can, that, works, so, he, succeed).

_____

Chapter 7

School Feeding Schemes Can Fill Children's Tummies and Farmers' Pockets

日本では当たり前の学校給食の効用をいま一度考えてみるにあたり、世界各地で行われている学校給食プログラムについて学んでみよう。また、地産地消という考え方が加わったときにどんな効果が生まれるだろう。

≫ Pre-reading Vocabulary Check

日本語の意味に合う英文になるよう適切なものを選びなさい。必要に応じて形を変えなさい。

・scheme　・feed　・reveal　・given　・prompt

1. 天気が良ければ、私たちはピクニックに出かける。

_____ good weather, we'll go on a picnic.

2. 犬に餌をあげた？

Have you _____ the dog?

3. 私たちにはその計画を遂行するのに十分な資本がない。

We don't have enough capital to carry the _____ through.

4. 彼の成功に促され、私も何か新しいことを始めようと思った。

His success _____ me to do something new.

5. その報告書は新しい販売戦略がうまくいっていることを明らかにしている。

The report _____ that the new marketing strategy works well.

≫ Reading Passage

🔊 Audio 14

1 Every day, about 370 million children worldwide benefit from national school feeding programmes*. Sometimes it's breakfast; sometimes it's lunch and sometimes it's both. But whatever the meal, school feeding

schemes are a nutritional lifeline for these children.

2 It's been proved repeatedly that being fed at school improves children's ₅ attendance and their academic performance. In Kenya, a breakfast programme increased school participation by 8.5% in a randomised control trial* of 25 pre-schools* School feeding schemes are also helping to greatly improve girls' access to primary education.

3 The African Union Commission* has recognised how important school ₁₀ meals are. In recent years, it's added another leg to this: pushing the idea that the schemes should be "home grown". This means that the food for these meals should be sourced* from local farmers. Getting local farmers involved in school feeding schemes has the potential to boost individuals' livelihoods and revitalise rural economies in Africa. ₁₅

4 Small-scale farmers – those who cultivate five or fewer acres of land – in Africa struggle to make ends meet. On their small plots they produce about 80% of the food that's consumed in Africa. Yet, most live in poverty.

5 One of the biggest problems they face is getting their produce to market. Main market centres tend to be far away from rural areas and ₂₀ transport is not even, given the poor state of infrastructure. As such, small-scale farmers have no choice but to rely on middlemen who tend to buy from them at lower prices than they'd earn at the markets themselves.

25 **6** It's this reality that's prompted the AU and others to call for governments to stock their school feeding programmes with locally grown produce.

7 Such initiatives make sense on a number of levels. Governments save money since the food doesn't have to be transported for long distances.

30 School children benefit from familiar, locally grown nutritious food. And the farmers themselves can use their earnings to support their families or even reinvest into their farming businesses.

8 Brazil's experience over the past few years suggests that homegrown school feeding programmes work. As of 2012 some 67% of its states and

35 municipalities were buying food produce from smallholder farmers for school feeding.

9 Inspired by the Brazilian experience, several African governments are integrating this pro-smallholder* procurement model into their school feeding schemes. For instance, the Purchase from Africans for Africa

40 initiative* is being piloted* in five countries: Ethiopia, Malawi, Mozambique, Niger and Senegal. Results from the first phase of implementation revealed that about 37% of participating farmers' produce was bought to support school meals.

NOTES

* **school feeding programmes**：学校給食プログラム (=school feeding schemes)
* **control trial**：対照試験
* **pre-schools**：幼稚園・保育園（未就学児が通う施設）
* **The African Union Commission**：アフリカ連合委員会（アフリカ連合 [the African Union, the AU] の一組織）
* **source**：(材料を) 調達する
* **pro-smallholder**：小自作農を支援している> pro-：…支持の
* **the Purchase from Africans for Africa initiative**：アフリカ自国食料購入プログラム
* **pilot**：試行する

>> Post-reading Vocabulary Check

➤ 日本語の意味に合う英文になるよう、次の中から適切な 動詞 を選び、必要に応じて形を変えなさい。

・benefit　・involve　・boost　・revitalise　・cultivate　・integrate

1. 初期の入植者はやせた土地を耕した。

The first settlers _____ the poor ground.

2. 芸術は瀬戸内海のコミュニティーを活性化するのに役立っている。

Art helps _____ communities on the Seto Inland sea.

3. 減税から恩恵を受けるのはお金持ちだけである。

Only rich people _____ from the tax reduction.

4. 彼女はいくつものプロジェクトに関わった。

She was _____ in a number of projects.

5. これらの国は EU の経済構造に組み込まれた。

These countries were _____ into the EU's economic structures.

6. 先生は生徒たちの自尊心を高めようとした。

The teacher tried to _____ students' self-esteem.

➤ 下記の 名詞 =英英・英日の語義が成立するように、空欄を埋めなさい。太字の名詞が空欄の場合は本文中から適切な単語を探して埋めましょう。

1. a □□□□□□□□□ = presence, [opposite] absence「出席 (率)」

2. potential = p □□□□□□□□□□「可能性」

3. l □□□□□□□□□ = source of income, means of support「生計」

4. produce = crops, p □□□□□□ s「農産物」

5. t □□□□□□□□ = transit, traffic「輸送」

6. i □□□□□□□□□□□□□ = the system of public works of a country, state, or region「インフラ、基幹施設」

7. municipality = t □□□, city「地方自治体」

8. i □□□□□□□□□□□□□□ = execution, realization「実施」

>> Comprehension Check True or False

下の英文が本文の内容として正しい場合は T、間違っている場合は F を選びましょう。

1. School meals are lifeline for some children.　　　　　　　　(T / F)

2. Brazil is a successful example of school feeding schemes.　　　(T / F)

3. Kenya participates in the Purchase from Africans for Africa initiative.　(T / F)

>> ACTIVE LEARNING for Discussion

➤ 給食も含め、日本におけるライフラインとしての子どもの食を守る取り組みの具体例を、ペアまたはグループであげてみましょう。

Example _____

_____

_____

➤ 地産地消（地元で作られた生産物を、その地域で消費すること）の具体例をあげて、ペアまたはグループでそのメリットを話し合ってみましょう。

Example _____

_____

_____

>> Comprehension Check Multiple Choice

本文の内容に照らして最も正しいものをa～cの中から選んで○をつけなさい。

1. Which of the following does NOT apply to what school feeding schemes have improved?

a. girls' access to primary education

b. children's academic performance

c. the state of infrastructure

2. Which of the following does NOT apply to the difficulties small-scale farmers face?

a. investment in their farming business

b. middlemen who buy from them at lower prices

c. a long distance to markets

3. Which of the following does NOT apply to the advantages of getting local farmers involved in school feeding schemes?

a. governments don't have to transport the food for long distances

b. children can learn agriculture

c. farmers can earn more money

>> English Composition for Idiom Learning   🔊 Audio 15

日本語の意味に合うよう、(　　　)内を並べ替えて英文を完成させましょう。並べ替え部分には本文中に登場するイディオムが含まれています。なお、文頭に来る語も小文字にしてあります。

1. ニューヨーク・シティでお金をやりくりして暮らすのは大変だ。

(make, is, hard, ends, it, to, meet) in New Yok City.

_____

2. 不景気のため、経営陣は工場を閉鎖するよりほかなかった。

Because of the recession, (choice, the, management, no, to, close, the, but, factories, had).

_____

3. この二つの問題が関わっていると考えることは道理にかなっている。

(subjects, it, are, sense, to, consider, makes, the, that, two, linked).

_____

Chapter 8

If You're Poor in America, You Can Be Both Overweight and Hungry

食べる物がたくさんあるから太る、食べる物がないから飢える、という極めて当たり前の論理が覆される状況がアメリカでは顕著である。それはなぜか、どのような悪循環がそこにはあるか、原因は何か探ってみよう。

≫ Pre-reading Vocabulary Check

日本語の意味に合う英文になるよう適切なものを選びなさい。必要に応じて形を変えなさい。

・overabundance　・contradiction　・poverty　・portion　・deprivation

1. 砂糖の過剰摂取は太るだけでなく、健康も損なってしまう。

The _____ of sugar isn't only making us fat but is also hurting our health.

2. 貧困は第三世界だけに存在するのではない。

_____ doesn't only exist in the Third World.

3. 彼女は三人前の食事を平らげた。

She ate a triple _____ of food.

4. 水の欠乏は脱水症として知られている。

The _____ of water is known as dehydration.

5. 「公平な税」は言葉の矛盾である。

"Fair taxes" is a _____ in terms.

≫ Reading Passage

≫ Audio 16

1 The U.S. is notorious for its weight problem. With just 5% of the world's population, it's home to 13% of the world's overweight and obese people. Roughly two-thirds of adults in the U.S. are overweight or obese

and, even more alarmingly, 38% of boys and girls ages 10 to 14 are.

2 At first glance, these numbers seem to reflect overabundance — Americans have more food than is good for them. But the problem is more complicated than that, and worse: Many of the same people who struggle with extra weight also regularly go to bed hungry. That may sound like an impossible contradiction, but dig deeper, and it quickly becomes clear how hunger and obesity are related. Both are often rooted in poverty.

3 Nearly 12% of American households are, by Agriculture Department* standards, "food insecure" — meaning they have difficulty buying enough safe and nutritious food to meet their household needs.

4 Food insecure adults in the U.S. are 32% more likely than others to be obese. Other studies suggest that food insecure children also tend to display significant behavioral problems,* disrupted social interactions, poor cognitive development* and marginal school performance. These challenges, in turn, increase their risk of becoming obese adults.

5 Poverty and unemployment have driven the dual rise in food insecurity and obesity since the 1960s, especially in rural America.

6 Food-insecure and low-income families face unique challenges that impair their ability to consume a healthful diet and maintain an ideal body weight. Their lifestyles tend to be sedentary because of their built environments,* and their food tends to be served in large portions. The

relatively inexpensive, calorie-dense food at their immediate disposal
often lacks the nutrients needed for optimal health. As a result, these are
punctuated by* cycles of financial and personal stress that lead to food
deprivation, overeating, limited access to health care, reduced
opportunities for physical activity and greater exposure to unhealthy food
environments.

7 How can such cycles be minimized? It will take a concerted effort from
many actors. The U.S. Congress should shift agriculture subsidies away
from their heavy focus on corn, soybeans and other Big Ag* crops and
toward the farming of fruits, vegetables, nuts and legumes.

8 It's also essential to
encourage more community
gardens and farmers markets,
subsidize healthy foods,
promote nutritious food
choices, and ban junk food
advertisements to children.
Fighting against obesity and
hunger is a matter of fighting
for basic food security – even
here in the U.S.

NOTES

* Agriculture Department：農務省
* behavioral problems：行動障害
* cognitive development：認知の発達
* built environments：人工的な環境
* be punctuated by ~：(主語の間に) ~がたびたび生じる
* Big Ag：巨大農業企業 (Ag は agriculture の略。アメリカでは農業はほぼ大規模化・企業化されており、例えば、「穀物メジャー」のアメリカ多国籍企業カーギルなどはその一例で、世界の農作物のシェアをこれらの少数の "Big Ag" が寡占している)

≫ Post-reading Vocabulary Check

➤ 日本語の意味に合う英文になるよう、次の中から適切な 動詞 を選び、必要に応じて形を変えなさい。

・disrupt　・impair　・consume　・subsidize　・ban　・minimize

1. 歩きタバコはニューヨークで禁じられている。

Smoking while walking is _____ in New York City.

2. 自分の家や車や職場での大気汚染を最小限に抑える方法がある。

There are ways you can _____ air pollution in your home, car or at work.

3. 雪のため、国内の多くの地域で交通機関が混乱した。

Snow has _____ public transport in many parts of the country.

4. 日本人は平均して年間約 55 キロの米を消費している。

The average Japanese _____ about 55 kg of rice annually.

5. 政府は低所得世帯向けの住居を助成している。

The government _____ housing for low-income families.

6. 大きな騒音は聴力を損なうこともある。

Loud noises can _____ your hearing.

➤ 下記の 形容詞または副詞 ＝英英・英日の語義が成立するように、空欄を埋めなさい。太字の形容詞または副詞が空欄の場合は本文中から適切な単語を探して埋めましょう。

1. notorious = i □□□□□□□ 「悪名高い」

2. obese = f □□, heavy 「肥満体の」

3. roughly = a □□□□□□□□□□□ 「ざっと」

4. a □□□□□□□□□ = frighteningly, shockingly 「驚くべきことに」

5. n □□□□□□□□ = healthy, wholesome 「栄養価の高い」

6. d □□□ = double, binary 「二重の」

7. r □□□□ = country, pastoral 「田舎の」

8. s □□□□□□□□ = sitting, inactive 「座りがちな、ほとんど体を動かさない」

9. o □□□□□□ = the most suitable 「最適な」

>> Comprehension Check — True or False

下の英文が本文の内容として正しい場合は T、間違っている場合は F を選びましょう。

1. About 66 % of adults in the U.S. are overweight or obese.　（ T / F ）

2. Poverty often results in both hunger and obesity.　（ T / F ）

3. Ban on junk food advertisements can worsen "food insecurity."　（ T / F ）

>> ACTIVE LEARNING for Keyword Check

本文に出てくる重要な単語についてペアまたはグループになって調べて表を完成させなさい。

用 語・テーマ	概 要
food insecurity フード・インセキュリティ／食の不安	
The difference between overweight and obesity 太り過ぎと肥満の違い	
to ban junk food advertisements to children ジャンクフードの子ども向け広告の禁止	

>> Comprehension Check Multiple Choice

本文の内容に照らして最も正しいものを a ～ c の中から選んで○をつけなさい。

1. Which of the following does NOT apply to what "food insecurity" is likely to cause?

  a. optimal health

  b. obesity

  c. overeating

2. Which of the following symptoms are "food insecure" children likely to show?

  a. great school performance

  b. positive social interaction

  c. poor cognitive development

3. Which of the following does the U.S. Congress subsidize heavily?

  a. Big Ag crops

  b. fruits

  c. vegetable

>> English Composition for Idiom Learning   ))) Audio 17

日本語の意味に合うよう、（　　　）内を並べ替えて英文を完成させましょう。並べ替え部分には本文中に登場するイディオムが含まれています。なお、文頭に来る語も小文字にしてあります。

1. 彼女の言うことを理解するのが多少難しい時がある。

  (have, I, some, understanding, difficulty, her).

_____

2. 一見したところ問題は簡単そうだ。

  (problem, first, at, the, glance, seems, easy).

_____

3. そのお金は彼の自由になる。

  (at, the, disposal, money, is, his).

_____

Chapter 9

This Supermarket Sells Only Wasted Food

日本でも食品廃棄物量の多さがたびたび話題に上がるが、その中でも、まだ食べられるのに捨ててしまう食品ロスをいかに減らすかにこそ、Chapter 8 の肥満と飢えをはじめとする現代の様々な問題解決への鍵があるのかもしれない。さらに、「モッタイナイ」精神から、食への関心も高められれば一石二鳥だろう。

≫ Pre-reading Vocabulary Check

日本語の意味に合う英文になるよう適切なものを選びなさい。必要に応じて形を変えなさい。

> ・customer　・restrictions　・due to　・amount　・stale

1. お医者さんは塩の使用量を減らすように私に言った。

The doctor told me to reduce the _____ of salt I used.

2. 古くなった野菜の匂いが充満していた。

A smell of _____ vegetables pervaded the air.

3. 日本では人々の移動の制限がない。

In Japan, there are no _____ on the movement of people.

4. お客様が第一です。

The _____ always comes first.

5. 試合は台風のために延期になった。

The game was put off _____ the typhoon.

≫ Reading Passage

🔊 Audio 18

1 Food waste is a big deal*: According to the United Nations' Food and Agriculture Organization*, 28 percent of the world's agriculture area is used to produce food that ultimately goes to waste each year. But now,

writes Feargus O'Sullivan for *CityLab**, a new supermarket stocked only with wasted food is tackling the problem head-on*. 5

2 The project is an outgrowth of British non-profit* the Real Junk Food Project, reports O'Sullivan. The group has long collected wasted food for pay-as-you-can cafés around the world, but its supermarket in Pudsey* takes the concept one step further. The market takes food that's donated by local restaurants and grocery stores and puts it on shelves to sell to 10 customers who pay what they can.

3 As Hazel Sheffield reports for *The Independent**, the store is already serving as a lifeline for families who are down on their luck. It's kind of like a food pantry, but has no restrictions on who gets the food. And the concept is not a new one: as Sheffield wrote in another report this month, 15 the idea has taken off in Denmark, too, due to a government initiative to reduce the country's volume of wasted food.

4 Last year, the USDA* launched its first-ever food waste reduction goal, aiming to reduce the amount of wasted food by 50 percent by 2030. The agency estimates that cutting just 15 percent of this waste in the 20 United States would provide enough food for more than 25 million Americans per year. And hunger isn't the only reason to reduce food waste: As Ben Schiller notes for *FastCo**, wasted food has a carbon dioxide impact equal to the output of one in four cars on the road

FOOD EDUCATION 食育

3

25 worldwide and consumes a quarter of the world's freshwater and 300 million barrels of oil each year.

5 Food waste supermarkets aren't the only weapon in the fight against waste: From activists working to improve the cachet of strange-looking fruits and veggies to craft beers made of wasted products like stale bread
30 and grapefruit, there are plenty of creative ways to buy and eat food that would otherwise be thrown out. Maybe it's time to bring the food waste supermarket concept to the United States – a delicious addition to the smorgasbord* of ways not to trash perfectly good meals.

NOTES

* **a big deal**：重大事（本書のタイトルにもなっている）
* **the United Nations' Food and Agriculture Organization**：FAO 国際連合食糧農業機関
* ***CityLab* (l. 4), *The Independent* (l. 12), *FastCo* (l. 23)**：いずれもニュース媒体
* **head-on**：真正面から
* **non-profit** = NPO, non-profit organization 非営利団体
* **Pudsey**：プジー（イギリス、ウェストヨークシャーの町）
* **the USDA** = the United States Department of Agriculture 米国農務省
* **smorgasbord**：スモーガスボード（スウェーデン語源の様々な料理を並べるビュッフェのスタイルの元になった料理名。そこから「寄せ集め」の意味にもなる）

≫ Post-reading Vocabulary Check

➤ 日本語の意味に合う英文になるよう、次の中から適切な 動詞 を選び、必要に応じて形を変えなさい。

> · tackle　· donate　· reduce　· launch　· improve　· trash

1. 我々は新しい時代の新しい難問に立ち向かうつもりだ。

We'll _____ the new challenges of the new era.

2. 多くの人々が社会環境を改善しようと努力してきた。

Many people have sought to _____ social conditions.

3. 近藤麻理恵は彼女の服を廃棄した。

Marie Kondo _____ her clothes.

4. 彼女は新しいビジネスを始めた。

She _____ her new business.

5. 彼は教会建設に全財産を寄付した。

He _____ his entire fortune to building churches.

6. 政府は軍事費を削減した。

The government _____ its military budget.

➤ 下記の 名詞 =英英・英日の語義が成立するように、空欄を埋めなさい。太字の名詞が空欄の場合
は本文中から適切な単語を探して埋めましょう。

1. o ☐☐☐☐☐☐☐☐ = consequence, by-product「派生物、副産物」

2. g ☐☐☐☐☐☐ = a shop that sells food and other things used in the home
「食料品店」

3. p ☐☐☐☐☐ = storage room「食料貯蔵庫」

4. initiative = p ☐☐☐, scheme, strategy「構想、戦略」

5. a ☐☐☐☐☐ = an administrative division「(政府の) 機関、局」

6. impact = effect, i ☐☐☐☐☐☐☐☐「影響」

7. w ☐☐☐☐☐ = a means of defending oneself in a conflict or contest
「対抗手段、武器」

>> Comprehension Check True or False

下の英文が本文の内容として正しい場合は T、間違っている場合は F を選びましょう。

1. We trash 28% of the food produced in the world each year. (T / F)
2. The concept of the supermarket in Pudsey is not new. (T / F)
3. There are supermarkets selling only food waste in the USA. (T / F)

>> ACTIVE LEARNING for Discussion

➤ 食料廃棄について日本の状況を調べて、グループで発表してみましょう。

- _____
- _____
- _____
- _____

➤ 第 5 パラグラフを参考にして食品廃棄を減らす方法を考えて、ペアまたはグループで話し合ってみましょう。

- _____
- _____
- _____
- _____

» Comprehension Check `Multiple Choice`

本文の内容に照らして最も正しいものを a ～ c の中から選んで○をつけなさい。

1. Which of the following is NOT true about the Real Junk Food Project?

    a. you can eat at its cafés even if you pay only £1

    b. its supermarket in Pudsey makes much profit

    c. its supermarket in Pudsey is pay-as-you-can

2. Which of the following does NOT apply to what would happen if we cut all the food waste?

    a. we would save a fourth of freshwater in the world each year

    b. we would save a lot of oil each year

    c. nobody would suffer from hunger

3. Which of the following is NOT likely to apply to the weapons in the fight against food waste?

    a. buying strange-looking grapefruits

    b. drinking beer made of local products

    c. eating dishes made of food waste

» English Composition for Idiom Learning

Audio 19

日本語の意味に合うよう、(　　　) 内を並べ替えて英文を完成させましょう。並べ替え部分には本文中に登場するイディオムが含まれています。なお、文頭に来る語も小文字にしてあります。

1. ワンガリ・マータイは考えをもう一歩先へ進め、「モッタイナイ」という考えを広めた。

Wangari Maathai (took, one, idea, the, step, further) and popularized the notion of "Mottainai."

_____

2. ツキに見放された彼女を見たくない。

(her, I, don't, see, want, to, down, on, luck, her).

_____

3. その計画は捨てていい。

(can, that, out, we, throw, scheme).

_____

Chapter 10 | The Missing Women in Workforce Data

女性は男性より労働に従事する割合が低いという見方は公平だろうか？ 筆者はインドの状況を具体例にとり、大きな見落としがあるとしてこれに異を唱える。従来の見方にどのような視点が欠けているのだろうか？

≫ Pre-reading Vocabulary Check

日本語の意味に合う英文になるよう適切なものを選びなさい。必要に応じて形を変えなさい。

・flawed ・ingredients ・poorly ・significantly ・jointly

1. 彼女の最初の小説は重大な欠点のある作品と言われている。

Her first novel is said to be a seriously _____ piece of work.

2. 事態は著しく改善した。

Things have improved _____.

3. 戦時中、子どもたちはあまり食事を与えられていなかった。

The children were _____ fed during the war.

4. 兄弟は車を共同で所有していた。

The brothers owned the car _____.

5. ボウルの中ですべての材料をよく混ぜなさい。

Mix all the _____ in a bowl.

≫ Reading Passage

🔊 Audio 20

1 There are serious inaccuracies in recording women's contribution to economic activity and estimating the proportion of women who are workers. While the census estimates male workers to be above 50 per

cent of the male population over several decades, the estimates of the proportion of female workers in the female population are unrealistically low.

2 The official statistics create the perception that the female work participation rate is very low in India – far lower than in most countries of the world. The fact is that women participate in the workforce to a far greater extent than is measured by the data. However, a lot of the work they do is unrecognised, invisible, uncounted and either unremunerated* or poorly remunerated.*

3 *Golgappa-Samosa example*

It is also argued that India's GDP would increase significantly if only the female work participation rate would increase and more women would work. The case of the *golgappas** or* *samosa** vendor described below shows why this argument is flawed.

4 When a male vendor sells *golgappas* or other snacks, he is able to do so because his wife wakes up early in the morning and spends six hours rolling out the *golgappas* and frying them or making all the other ingredients that get loaded onto the cart that the vendor takes to different localities to sell. The value of the *golgappas* gets counted in the GDP. This value includes the labour contributed by both husband and wife.

5 However, the problem is that while he gets counted as a worker, his wife does not.

6 The tragedy is that neither she herself nor her husband sees her as a worker or considers her contribution as valuable.

7 If her husband says she only does housework and she says "*kuch nahin karti*" (I do nothing), she will not get counted as a worker in the official statistics.

8 This applies equally to women's contribution to agriculture, animal husbandry, collection and processing of non-timber forest produce* and other products that are "jointly" produced within the family. It took hours of discussions with men and women in a village in Rajasthan,* during which I recounted activity with contributions by women to agriculture, before the men accepted that their spouse was also a worker and contributed at least 50 per cent of the value of the output produced on the farm.

> **NOTES**
>
> * **unremunerated / remunerated**：（労働に対して）報酬を支払われてない／報酬を支払われている
>
> * ***golgappa***：ゴールガッパー（中が空洞になっている一口サイズの球状をした、小麦粉の生地を揚げたインドの菓子）
>
> * **or**：すなわち
>
> * **samosa**：サモサ（油で揚げたスナック。ここではゴールガッパーよりも一般的に知られているサモサで言い換えられている）
>
> * **non-timber forest produce**：非木材林産物、NTFPs（木材を伐採する方法で森林を利用するのではなく、植物（例えば、きのこや樹脂）や動物を採集する方法で森林を利用することに主眼を置いた概念である）
>
> * **Rajasthan**：ラジャスタン（インドの西北部の地方）

» Post-reading Vocabulary Check

➤ 日本語の意味に合う英文になるよう、次の中から適切な 動詞 を選び、必要に応じて形を変えなさい。

・estimate　・apply　・measure　・load　・contribute　・recount

1. 彼は刑務所で経験したことを詳しく話した。

He _____ his experiences in prison.

2. 私たちは子どもたちの成績をどのように測るべきか話し合ってきた。

We have discussed how we should _____ children's performance.

3. 港湾労働者は貨物を積んだり下ろしたりする。

Dock workers _____ and discharge cargo.

4. 彼は医学の発展に大いに貢献した。

He _____ a great deal to the development of medicine.

5. その議論はこの場合に当てはまる。

The argument _____ in this case.

6. その修理工は修理代を 1000 ドルと見積もった。

The repairperson _____ the cost of repairs at $1000.

➤ 下記の 名詞 ＝英英・英日の語義が成立するように、空欄を埋めなさい。太字の名詞が空欄の場合は本文中から適切な単語を探して埋めましょう。

1. inaccuracy = e □□□□ 「誤り」

2. p □□□□□□□□ = ratio, relative amount/number 「割合」

3. c □□□□□ = an official count or survey, especially of a population 「国勢調査」

4. w □□□□□□□□ = workers, human resources 「労働人口」

5. p □□□□□□□□ = realization, awareness 「認識」

6. v □□□□□ = a person offering something for sale in the street 「行商人、露天商人」

7. t □□□□□□ = disaster, calamity 「悲劇」

8. s □□□□□ = husband or wife, partner 「配偶者」

9. output = p □□□□□□□□□□ 「生産高」

>> Comprehension Check `True or False`

下の英文が本文の内容として正しい場合は T、間違っている場合は F を選びましょう。

1. According to the census, more than half of Indian women are working.

(T / F)

2. In India, female workers are often unpaid.   (T / F)

3. According to the author, the wives' contribution to the farm is as much as their husbands' in Rajasthan.   (T / F)

>> ACTIVE LEARNING for Discussion

➤ あなたの身の回りで公式にはカウントされていない「労働」はありますか。ペアまたはグループで意見を出し合ってみましょう。

・ _____

・ _____

・ _____

➤ インドにおいて公式にはカウントされていない「女性の労働」が可視化されれば、女性の地位や権利などの点でどのような違いが生まれると考えますか。ペアまたはグループで話し合ってみましょう。

・ _____

・ _____

・ _____

>> Comprehension Check Multiple Choice

本文の内容に照らして最も正しいものを a ～ c の中から選んで○をつけなさい。

1. Which of the following does NOT apply to the reasons why Indian women aren't counted as workers?

   a. because their husbands don't see them as workers

   b. because they don't see themselves as workers

   c. because their housework is not valuable

2. Which of the following thinks that the female work participation rate is not as low as it is generally thought to be?

   a. the author

   b. the census takers

   c. Indian women

3. Which of the following applies to what the official statistics are likely to count as labour?

   a. raising children

   b. selling *golgappas*

   c. frying *golgappas*

>> English Composition for Idiom Learning   🔊 Audio 21

日本語の意味に合うよう、(   ) 内を並べ替えて英文を完成させましょう。並べ替え部分には本文中に登場するイディオムが含まれています。なお、文頭に来る語も小文字にしてあります。

1. 多くの学生が海外でのボランティア活動に参加している。

   (many, abroad, students, in, volunteer, participate, activities).

   _____

2. 両親は子どもたちをある程度信頼している。

   The parents (extent, children, to, their, some, trust).

   _____

3. 彼女はその話を認めもしなければ、否定もしなかった。

   (she, confirmed, denied, the, nor, story, neither).

   _____

Chapter 11 | Saudi Women Join the Workforce as Country Reforms

男女同席が禁止されているイスラム圏のサウジ・アラビアでは、女性はどのように働いているのだろうか。最新の動向を見てみよう。

>> Pre-reading Vocabulary Check

日本語の意味に合う英文になるよう適切なものを選びなさい。必要に応じて形を変えなさい。

- implicit · lately · burdens · strategy · provided

1. これらは彼女にのしかかる家計上の負担である。

These are financial _____ on her.

2. 彼らは互いに支持しあうという暗黙の了解があった。

They had an _____ agreement that they would support each other.

3. その会社は有効な競争戦略を立てた。

The company developed a workable _____ for competitiveness .

4. このところ自体が好転してきた。

Things have become better _____.

5. 天気さえ良ければ、行きます。

I will go, _____ that the weather is fine.

>> Reading Passage

🔊 Audio 22

■ "Implicit" acceptance of gender mixing

For years labor laws in Saudi Arabia prevented gender mixing* in the workplace. But "lately, there has been an implicit and unofficial acceptance of gender mixing in the work environment here," says Bader

Aljalajel, who opened his coffee shop, 12 Cups, in one of Riyadh's new ₅
glitzy boulevards in 2016.

2 The shop is manned* by five male Saudi
baristas and some expats.* Aljalajel now plans
to open a second shop, this time staffed* by
female baristas. ₁₀

3 "Women who sent us their applications
know that they will deal with men at work,"
says Aljalajel. "Those who have an issue with
that will become the black sheep."

4 The laws have been trending in this ₁₅
direction for years. In 2011, a law was passed
that all shops selling women-related products,
such as lingerie, should only have female sales
representatives. In 2016, drug stores and optics shops could request
permits to hire Saudi women, too, so long as the female staff remained ₂₀
separate from male workers and customers.

5 The Saudi Vision 2030* strategy, set by Saudi Crown Prince
Mohammed Bin Salman*, aims to increase female participation in the
workforce from 22% now to 30% in all sectors in 2030.

6 "There are now 600,000 Saudi women working for the private sector, ₂₅
30,000 of whom joined the market last September and October," says
Khaled Abalkhail, a spokesman for the Ministry of Labor and Social
Development. "This figure stood at 90,000 Saudi women only back in
2011."

7 Women no longer a burden ₃₀

While more Saudi women are entering the private sector, the challenge is persuading them to stay there.

8 "From our experience, four out of 10 women leave the jobs that we secure for them a few months after joining because their families asked them to," says Redwan Aljelwah, who in 2016 founded Riyadh-based recruitment consultancy, Mada, which operates in the retail, F&B,* and IT sectors.

9 Furthermore, Aljelwah says that demand for female employees remains much lower than for males. The unemployment rate* for Saudi women in the third quarter* of 2016, the most recent figures available, was 34.5%.

10 "All sectors are open to Saudi women, provided that they secure them a safe working environment," says Khaled Abalkhail, a spokesman for the Ministry of Labor and Social Development.* He added that the Ministry of Labor and Social Development runs courses to teach Saudi women soft and hard professional skills* to help them find jobs.

11 "When women work, they are no longer looked upon as burdens that their families have to bear until they get married." adds Aljalajel, "They have the option to become independent."

NOTES

* **gender mixing**：男女同席
* **man**：（動）店員を配置する
* **expats** = expatriates 外国人
* **staff**：（動）（スタッフ等を）配置する
* **the Saudi Vision 2030**：ビジョン 2030（石油依存型経済から脱却し、投資収益に基づく国家建設を目指す経済改革計画）
* **Saudi Crown Prince Mohammed Bin Salman**：サウジの皇太子ムハンマド・ビン・サルマーン
* **F&B** = food & beverage 飲食業界
* **unemployment rate**：失業率（職に就く意思があるのに見つけることができない労働者の割合）
* **quarter**：四半期（1 年を 4 等分した期間）
* **the Ministry of Labor and Social Development**：労働社会発展省
* **soft and hard professional skill**：専門的なソフトスキルとハードスキル（ソフトスキルとは、対人的な交渉・指導・意思疎通がスムーズに行える能力で、それに対してハードスキルとは体系だった知識を使いこなす能力のことを指す）

» Post-reading Vocabulary Check

➤ 日本語の意味に合う英文になるよう、次の中から適切な 動詞 を選び、必要に応じて形を変えなさい。

> ・prevent　・deal　・aim　・persuade　・secure　・bear

1. 地震の際、我々はまず緊急交通ルートの確保をした。

In the earthquake we first _____ emergency transportation routes.

2. 各メンバーが各々の費用を負担する。

Each member _____ one's share of the cost.

3. 私たちはいつも商品を改良しようと努めています。

We always _____ to improve our products.

4. それらの規則は事故を妨げることを目的としている。

The rules are designed to _____ accidents.

5. 私は気難しい顧客を扱うのが得意ではありません。

I'm not good at _____ with difficult customers.

6. 彼女は彼にその申し出を受けるように説得した。

She _____ him to accept the offer

➤ 下記の 名詞 ＝英英・英日の語義が成立するように、空欄を埋めなさい。太字の名詞が空欄の場合は本文中から適切な単語を探して埋めましょう。

1. boulevard = avenue, s □□□□□ 「大通り」

2. b □□□□ s □□□□ = a member of a family or group who is regarded as a disgrace to them 「厄介者」

3. sales r □□□□□□□□□□□□ = sales people 「販売員」

4. optics shop = g □□□□□□ shop 「眼鏡店」

5. p □□□□□ = authorization 「許可」

6. sector = c □□□□□□, enterprise 「企業」

7. r □□□□□ = the sale of goods to the public in relatively small quantities for use 「小売業」

8. option = c □□□□□ 「選択肢」

>> Comprehension Check **True or False**

下の英文が本文の内容として正しい場合は T、間違っている場合は F を選びましょう。

1. Gender mixing is being accepted openly in Saudi Arabia. (T / F)

2. Crown Prince Mohammed Bin Salman encourages all sectors to hire Saudi women. (T / F)

3. About one-third of the Saudi women who were available for work were unemployed in 2016. (T / F)

>> ACTIVE LEARNING for Discussion

宗教や習慣が女性の労働人口への参入を困難にしている例をあげて、ペアまたはグループで話し合ってみましょう。

- _____

- _____

- _____

- _____

- _____

- _____

- _____

- _____

- _____

- _____

>> Comprehension Check Multiple Choice

本文の内容に照らして最も正しいものを a 〜 c の中から選んで○をつけなさい。

1. Which of the following don't work in the coffee shop 12 Cups?

　a. male Saudi baristas

　b. female Saudi baristas

　c. foreigners

2. It is legal for Saudi women to work in

　a. gender mixing optics shops.

　b. lingerie shops.

　c. 12 Cups.

3. Which of the following prevents Saudi women from keeping working?

　a. family members' oppositions

　b. the high unemployment rate

　c. the labor laws in Saudi Arabia

>> English Composition for Idiom Learning   🔊 Audio 23

日本語の意味に合うよう、（　　　）内を並べ替えて英文を完成させましょう。並べ替え部分には本文中に登場するイディオムが含まれています。なお、文頭に来る語も小文字にしてあります。

1. 私は上司に対して問題を抱えています。

(having, an, my, issue, I'm, with, boss).

_____

2. 静かにしてくれさえすれば、ここに居てもいいですよ。

You can stay here, (long, as, so, keep, you, quiet).

_____

3. 失敗は学ぶ機会と見なされている。

(to, failure, is, opportunity, upon, as, an, looked, learn).

_____

Chapter 12

Migrant Workers in Thailand Live Harsh, But Improving, Reality

東南アジアの他の国々が経済発展を遂げるにつれて、タイの移民労働政策も変更を迫られている。外国人出稼ぎ労働者の日常風景と、タイの移民労働政策の歴史と現在を見てみよう。

≫ Pre-reading Vocabulary Check

日本語の意味に合う英文になるよう適切なものを選びなさい。必要に応じて形を変えなさい。

> ・migrant　・dependence　・manufacturing　・design　・legislation

1. 過重労働を強いられ、給料が未払いだと主張する外国人出稼ぎ労働者に BBC が話を聞いた。

The BBC spoke to _____ workers who claimed they were overworked and underpaid.

2. 新しい政策はフレックスタイム制の導入を可能にすることを目的としている。

The new policies are _____ to enable the introduction of flexible working hours.

3. アメリカ合衆国議会はいくつかの法律を可決した。

The US Congress approved several pieces of _____.

4. 日本の製造業は 1980 年代から空洞化している。

The Japanese _____ industry has been hollowing out since the 1980s.

5. 我々はエネルギー源としての石油への依存を減らすべきである。

We should reduce our _____ on oil as a source of energy.

Children play in a village built from shipping containers that house migrant workers on the outskirts of Bangkok. About 700 people live in the settlement's 120 metal boxes. (Photo by Akira Kodaka)

>> Reading Passage

 Audio 24

1 BANGKOK – The clusters of yellow shipping containers* sitting on a bleak parcel of land on the dusty outskirts of Bangkok are a symbol of Thailand's growing dependence on migrant workers.

2 Children play among the containers, shouting in Cambodian and Thai. The makeshift* village in the city's Bangphlat district* is home to around 700 migrant workers from Cambodia, Laos and Myanmar.

3 Each container has only about 4.5 sq. meters* of space. But the rudimentary housing is free; there is even a school for the children.

4 One 24-year-old Cambodian, Noi Yingmeemaoi has been working in Thailand since she was 12 years old. She left Cambodia when her farming family became mired in debt. She married a Thai man working at the same construction site, partly because she wanted her children "to have Thai nationality and enjoy a prosperous life in Thailand."

5 Thailand's vibrant economy and rising living standards attract legions of workers from its poorer neighbors. The migrants are a valuable source of labor for Thailand, which began industrializing rapidly in the 1980s, helped by foreign investment and a resource boom.* The country's economic development pulled Thai workers out of farming, fishing and construction and into manufacturing.

6 As the Southeast Asian country's economy took off, labor markets became tight and migrant workers filled the gap. Now, more than 3.3 million foreign nationals work in Thailand and make up 10% of its

5

10

15

20

workforce. As the country ages, it is growing increasingly dependent on foreign labor.

25 **7** But now that Thailand's neighbors are also developing rapidly, there are more good jobs at home. That makes fishery and construction work in Thailand less attractive. Many residents of the container village say they do not want their children to do the same kind of jobs they do.

8 The growing competition for labor has spurred Thailand to take steps

30 to retain foreign workers. Since 2017, the government has enacted a series of laws to accept immigrants and crack down on human trafficking* and forced labor.*

9 The move was aimed mainly at defusing international criticism about rampant human rights violations in the country's lightly regulated labor

35 market. But it was also designed to improve migrants' working conditions to ensure that they stay in the country.

10 The new legislation requires employers to take steps to provide legal status to migrants working without a visa or proper identification.

11 Noi Yingmeemaoi is a beneficiary of the new rules. "I no longer have

40 to worry about being detained* and deported,* " she said.

"Migrant workers in Thailand live harsh, but improving, reality—Bangkok takes legal steps to retain vital laborers from neighboring countries" by YUKAKO ONO, Nikkei staff writer, *Nikkei Asian Review* (February 17, 2019)

© 1000 Words / Shutterstock.com, PHUKET TOWN, THAILAND. Migrant workers sit in the back of a pick-up truck on their way to a construction site.

NOTES

* **shipping containers**：輸送用コンテナ
* **Bangphlat district**：バーンプラット区
* **resource boom**：天然資源ブーム
* **forced labor**：強制労働
* **deport**：本国送還する

* **makeshift**：間に合わせの
* **sq. meters** = square meters 平方メートル
* **human trafficking**：人身売買
* **detain**：拘束する

≫ Post-reading Vocabulary Check

➤ 日本語の意味に合う英文になるよう、次の中から適切な 動詞 を選び、必要に応じて形を変えなさい。

・industrialize　・age　・spur　・retain　・regulate　・ensure

1. 政府は過度な大気汚染を規制した。

The government _____ excessive air pollution.

2. 小さい樽の方がより早くウイスキーを熟成する。

Smaller barrels _____ the whiskey more quickly.

3. 日本は高度に工業化された国である。

Japan is a highly _____ country.

4. 主力となる従業員を引き止めておくのはビジネスを成功させる上で重要である。

_____ key employees is critical to the success of your business.

5. 政府は生産者に対して、価格が安定するように十分な量を供給するように求めている。

The government is calling on producers to provide adequate supplies to _____ that prices are stable.

6. 先生は子供たちがもっと勉強するように駆り立てた。

The teacher _____ the children to study harder.

➤ 下記の 形容詞または副詞 ＝英英・英日の語義が成立するように、空欄を埋めなさい。太字の形容詞または副詞が空欄の場合は本文中から適切な単語を探して埋めましょう。

1. b ☐☐☐☐ = desert, open「殺風景な、わびしい」

2. rudimentary = s ☐☐☐☐☐, basic「原始的な、基本の」

3. p ☐☐☐☐☐☐☐☐☐ = thriving, flourishing「豊かな」

4. v ☐☐☐☐☐☐ = energetic, vigorous「活気のある」

5. valuable = p ☐☐☐☐☐☐☐, expensive「貴重な」

6. rampant = overabundantly w ☐☐☐☐☐☐☐☐☐「まん延した」

7. proper= official, f ☐☐☐☐☐「正式の」

8. l ☐☐☐☐ = lawful, official「法的な、合法の」

>> Comprehension Check | True or False

下の英文が本文の内容として正しい場合は T、間違っている場合は F を選びましょう。

1. Migrant workers enabled Thailand to industrialize in the 1980s. (T / F)
2. Many inhabitants of the container village hope that their children will lead better lives. (T / F)
3. Noi Yingmeemaoi used to worry about being detained and deported. (T / F)

>> ACTIVE LEARNING for Discussion

➤ 日本における移民（外国人）労働者に関するニュースを探してきて、グループで発表しましょう。

_____

_____

_____

_____

➤ 最初の設問で探してきたニュースや、タイの移民労働政策を踏まえて、今後日本の移民労働政策がどのようにあるべきかペアまたはグループで話し合ってみましょう。

_____

_____

_____

_____

>> Comprehension Check Multiple Choice

本文の内容に照らして最も正しいものをa～cの中から選んで○をつけなさい。

1. Which of the following applies to the industry more Thais have engaged in since the 1980s?

   a. construction

   b. fishery

   c. manufacturing

2. Which of the following is the most likely reason why the competition for labor has been growing in Thailand?

   a. economic development of neighboring countries

   b. increasingly dependent on migrant workers

   c. human rights violations in the labor market

3. Which of the following has the Thai government been cracking down on since 2017?

   a. illegal foreign workers

   b. human trafficking

   c. migrants without visas

>> English Composition for Idiom Learning

🔊 Audio 25

日本語の意味に合うよう、（　　　）内を並べ替えて英文を完成させましょう。並べ替え部分には本文中に登場するイディオムが含まれています。なお、文頭に来る語も小文字にしてあります。

1. もう東京に住んでいるので、昔の友達に会うことはない。

   (that, I, I, never, live, in, now, see, my, friends, old, Tokyo).

   _____

2. 我々は家庭内暴力への対策を講じる。

   (take, steps, violence, we, address, domestic, to).

   _____

3. 警察はホリデー・シーズンには飲酒運転を厳しく取り締まる。

   (drunk, police, crack, down, on, the, driving) in the holiday season.

   _____

Chapter 13 | A Modern History of the Ogasawara Islands: Migration, Diversity, and War

>> Pre-reading Vocabulary Check

日本語の意味に合う英文になるよう適切なものを選びなさい。必要に応じて形を変えなさい。

· diversity   · height   · supplies   · sovereignty   · setback

1. 彼らはそれらの諸島をアルゼンチンの主権へ返還することを拒否した。

They refused to transfer the islands back to Argentine _____.

2. わが大学は多様性を誇りにしている。

Our university is proud of its _____.

3. 海軍はその地震のあと救援物資をメキシコに送った。

The Navy delivered disaster-relief _____ to Mexico after the earthquake.

4. 彼は自分の失敗を受け止めた。

He accepted his _____.

5. これらの作家全員、1920 年代には流行の極みにいた。

All these writers were the _____ of fashion in the 1920s.

>> Reading Passage

🔊 **Audio 26**

1 Until the early nineteenth century, the islands were uninhabited, although people occasionally stopped there for short periods. Permanent settlement began in 1830, when a group of around 25 men and women

東京都に属する小笠原諸島は、主要な島である父島まで東京の竹芝ターミナル
から船で丸一日かかる。その小笠原諸島が多様性に満ちた歴史を持つことは
知っているだろうか。その始まりを見てみよう。

from Oahu in the Hawaiian Islands arrived in Chichijima in the expectation of growing demand for commerce. The first settlers were a mixture of Europeans, North Americans, native Hawaiians, and other Pacific Islanders*.

2 The first inhabitants farmed vegetables, grains, and potatoes, raised livestock, and fished for sea turtles. They supplemented their livelihood by selling fresh food to sailors who used the islands as a stopping point during long ocean voyages.

3 The early to mid-nineteenth century was the height of the whaling industry throughout the Pacific, driven by demand for oil for lamps. In the 1820s, whalers from the United States began to expand into the northwestern Pacific, but with Japan still isolated under the Tokugawa shōguns, finding safe harbors in which to replenish supplies in Japan or the Ryūkyū Islands* was not easy. The Bonin Islands* therefore made an attractive place for large ships to stop and replenish supplies.

4 For around half a century after the first settlers arrived, the Ogasawara Islands were not under the formal sovereignty of any nation. In the 1850s, Matthew Perry, commander of the US Navy's East India Squadron,* passed by Chichijima with his famous fleet of "black ships" on his way to Uraga and planned to incorporate the islands as US territory.

5 In the 1860s, the shogunate* sent a delegation* with the legendary castaway John Manjirō as interpreter in an attempt to claim the islands as Japanese territory. But attempts to settle the islands from Japan met with setbacks and were soon abandoned.

30 **6** In the years that followed, a diverse range of people arrived on the two main islands: deserting sailors who fled harsh conditions by jumping ship while in port, people forced to land because of illness or injury, shipwreck survivors, and pirates who came ashore intent on robbing the islanders of their money or women.

35 **7** The islanders' ethnic backgrounds were similarly diverse, reflecting the origins of sailors on whaling vessels at the time: alongside Europeans, there were people from islands all around the Pacific, Indian, and Atlantic Oceans.

8 The Ogasawara Islands were on the front lines of the globalization
40 taking place throughout the Pacific in the nineteenth century, as sailors came ashore and settled down. The islands were an autonomous space that encapsulated* in miniature* the global society of the time.

NOTES

* **Pacific Islanders**：太平洋諸島の住民（特にポリネシア人を指す）
* **the Ryūkyū Islands**：琉球諸島（奄美群島、沖縄諸島、宮古列島、八重山列島の総体）
* **the Bonin Islands**：ボニン諸島（小笠原諸島の別名。無人島<ruby>無人島<rt>ぶにんのしま</rt></ruby>と呼ばれていたことに由来）
* **East India Squadron**：東インド戦艦
* **shogunate**：幕府
* **delegation**：派遣団
* **encapsulate**：カプセルに包む、要約する
* **miniature**：ミニチュア

»» Post-reading Vocabulary Check

➤ 日本語の意味に合う英文になるよう、次の中から適切な 動詞 を選び、必要に応じて形を変えなさい。

・supplement　・expand　・incorporate　・abandon　・flee　・settle

1. 子どもは食事にビタミンやミネラルを補う必要がある。

Children need to _____ their diets with vitamins or minerals.

2. 多くの作家や芸術家が 1920 年代に国を捨ててパリへ逃げた。

Many writers and artists _____ the country for Paris in the 1920s.

3. その村は市に組み入れられた。

The village was _____ into the city.

4. 彼らはバンコクの近くに落ち着いた。

They have _____ down near Bangkok.

5. タイとの貿易は着実に拡大している。

Our trade with Thailand is steadily _____.

6. 政府はその改革案を断念した。

The government _____ the reform plan.

➤ 下記の 形容詞または副詞 ＝英英・英日の語義が成立するように、空欄を埋めなさい。太字の形容詞または副詞が空欄の場合は本文中から適切な単語を探して埋めましょう。

1. occasionally = s □□□□□□□, from time to time「時おり」

2. p □□□□□□□□ = everlasting, eternal「永続的な」

3. i □□□□□□□ = remote, lonely「隔絶した、孤立した」

4. l □□□□□□□ = famous, popular「伝説的な」

5. diverse = v □□□□□□「多様な」

6. h □□□□ = cruel, severe「過酷な」

7. ashore = on to the □□□□「陸上へ」

8. s □□□□□□□□ = likewise, in the same way「同様に」

9. a □□□□□□□□□ = independent, self-governing「自律性の」

» Comprehension Check　True or False

下の英文が本文の内容として正しい場合は T、間違っている場合は F を選びましょう。

1. The Ogasawara Islands were US territory in the 1850s. 　　　　（ T / F ）

2. Some came ashore to rob Ogasawara Islanders of their money. 　（ T / F ）

3. The Ogasawara Islands were a global society in the 19th century. （ T / F ）

»　ACTIVE LEARNING for Keyword Check & Planning

➤ 本文に出てくる重要な単語についてペアまたはグループになって調べて表を完成させなさい。

用　語・テーマ	概　要
John Manjirō ジョン万次郎	

➤ 小笠原村観光協会の HP を調べて、架空の小笠原諸島旅行の予定を立ててみましょう。
　（https://www.ogasawaramura.com）

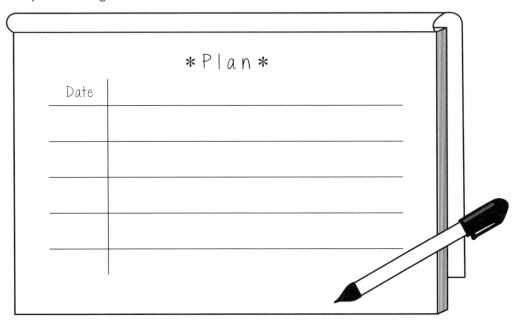

＊Ｐｌａｎ＊

Date

≫ Comprehension Check Multiple Choice

本文の内容に照らして最も正しいものを a 〜 c の中から選んで○をつけなさい。

1. Which of the following does NOT apply to the first settlers' livelihoods?

    a. farming

    b. ocean voyage

    c. selling fresh food

2. Which of the following brought the whaling industry boom in the 1800s?

    a. demand for commerce

    b. demand for fresh food

    c. demand for lamp oil

3. Which of the following is NOT true about John Manjirô?

    a. he worked for the shogunate

    b. he got lost in the sea

    c. he came back to Japan with Commander Perry

≫ English Composition for Idiom Learning

 Audio 27

日本語の意味に合うよう、（　　　）内を並べ替えて英文を完成させましょう。並べ替え部分には本文中に登場するイディオムが含まれています。なお、文頭に来る語も小文字にしてあります。

1. 彼は少年を救助しようと海へ飛び込んだ。

    (in, sea, he, save, the, boy, an, attempt, to, jumped, into, the).

    _____

2. 幹部は経費削減に熱心である。

    (the, are, intent, executives, on, costs, cutting).

    _____

3. ニューヨーク・ファッション・ウィークは 9 月に開催される。

    (in, New, Fashion, York, will, place, September, take, Week).

    _____

Chapter 14 | Reggae Officially Declared Global Cultural Treasure

2018 年、ジャマイカの音楽「レゲエ」がユネスコによって無形文化遺産として世界遺産登録された。どのような歴史を持つのか、なぜ世界遺産に登録されるに至ったのか探ってみよう。

>> Pre-reading Vocabulary Check

日本語の意味に合う英文になるよう適切なものを選びなさい。必要に応じて形を変えなさい。

· export   · discourse   · vehicle   · means   · discrimination

1. 目的は手段を正当化する（うそも方便）。

The end justifies the _____.

2. 砂糖はジャマイカの主要輸出品である。

Sugar is the major _____ of Jamaica.

3. 彼女たちは女性差別と戦った。

They fought against _____ against women.

4. 彼女は宣伝活動の手段としてマスコミを利用した。

She used the press as a _____ for her propaganda.

5. みんな環境に関する真剣な議論に関わるべきだ。

Everybody should engage in serious environmental _____.

>> Reading Passage

 Audio 28

I UNESCO*, the United Nations' cultural agency, inscribed the "uniquely Jamaican" musical tradition into its collection of important cultural practices from around the world.

© Debbie Ann Powell / Shutterstock.com
Coral Cliff Gaming and Entertainment on Jimmy Cliff Boulevard in Montego Bay, Jamaica

2 While many of the cultural practices on the list are truly ancient, reggae as an artform only emerged in the 1960s but has gone on to become, arguably, Jamaica's No. 1 cultural export as well as an international musical language.

3 "While in its embryonic state Reggae music was the voice of the marginalized, the music is now played and embraced by a wide cross-section of society, including various genders, ethnic and religious groups. Its contribution to international discourse on issues of injustice, resistance, love and humanity underscores the dynamics of the element as being at once cerebral, socio-political, sensual and spiritual," the UN says in a statement. "The basic social functions of the music – as a vehicle for social commentary, a cathartic practice, and a means of praising God – have not changed, and the music continues to act as a voice for all."

4 The recognition is a welcome one. Laurence Cane-Honeysett, author of a book about the influential U.K.-based reggae label Trojan Records, calls the inscription an "amazingly positive" move in an interview of the *Guardian*. "The impact and influence of the genre globally has long been overlooked," Cane-Honeysett says. "It has contributed significantly to the development of multiculturalism, with ska, rock steady and reggae of the 1960s and early '70s having a notably positive effect in the breaking down of social barriers by bringing together people of all colors, particularly in Britain."

5 Reggae's rise and global success is especially remarkable considering its origins. The music grew out of earlier popular styles in Jamaica, ska

© Ben Houdijk / Shutterstock.com
Toots & the Maytals, TivoliVredenburg, Utrecht, The Netherlands

© catwalker / Shutterstock.com

and rock steady. Reggae combined these styles with highly politicized lyrics by poor musicians, mainly in the capital city of Kingston, to create
30 style of music that spoke for the downtrodden, calling for social change. For that reason, it attracted followers of the Rastafarian movement, which has its roots in Jamaica. The community believes in the divinity of Ethiopian emperor Haile Selassie I,* who was crowned in 1930, among its other tenets, and followers faced discrimination by police and public, both
35 in pre- and post- British colonial rule. In Jamaica, the Rastafarian community lives by a set of dietary guidelines and grows marijuana* for sacramental* use. Many popular reggae songwriters, most notably Bob Marley,* spread Rastafarian messages and iconography across the world through their music.

NOTES

* **UNESCO**：ユネスコ（国際連合教育科学文化機関）
* **Haile Selassie I**：ハイレ・セラシエ 1 世（1892-1975）（エチオピア皇帝［在位 1930-74］）
* **marijuana**：マリファナ
* **sacramental**：聖餐用の
* **Bob Marley**：ボブ・マーリー（1945-1981）（レゲエ・ミュージシャン）

≫ Post-reading Vocabulary Check

➤ 日本語の意味に合う英文になるよう、次の中から適切な 動詞 を選び、必要に応じて形を変えなさい。

・inscribe ・emerge ・underscore ・combine ・politicize ・crown

1. 彼らは彼女の名前を寄贈者として名簿に載せた。

They ＿＿＿＿＿ her name as a donor.

2. 都会の警察署はかなり政治色を帯びる傾向にあった。

Urban police departments tended to be highly ＿＿＿＿＿.

3. 食事療法は運動と結びつけたらとても効果がある。

Diets are very effective when ＿＿＿＿＿ with exercise.

4. 女王は 30 年前に王位についた。

The Empress was ＿＿＿＿＿ thirty years ago.

5. 二つの対立する意見が議論のなかで浮上した。

Two contrary opinions ＿＿＿＿＿ in the discussion.

6. 彼はその問題の重要性を強調した。

He ＿＿＿＿＿ the importance of the problem.

➤ 下記の 形容詞または副詞 ＝英英・英日の語義が成立するように、空欄を埋めなさい。太字の形容詞または副詞が空欄の場合は本文中から適切な単語を探して埋めましょう。

1. a □□□□□□ = of long ago, classical「古来の」

2. a □□□□□□□ = possibly, probably「ほぼ間違いなく」

3. embryonic = b □□□□□□□□, elementary「初期の」

4. s □□□□□□ = physical, bodily, animal「官能的な、肉感的な」

5. globally = w □□□□□□□□「世界的に」

6. n □□□□□□ = impressively, especially「著しく、特に」

7. r □□□□□□□□□ = extraordinary, outstanding「注目すべき、著しい」

>> Comprehension Check True or False

下の英文が本文の内容として正しい場合は T、間違っている場合は F を選びましょう。

1. UNESCO highly appreciates Reggae.   (T / F)

2. Reggae is very ancient.   (T / F)

3. Haile Selassie was the emperor in Jamaica.   (T / F)

>> ACTIVE LEARNING for Discussion

➤ Bob Marley & The Wailers の曲 "One Love/ People Get Ready" を探して聞いてみましょう。

➤ "One Love/ People Get Ready" の歌詞を探して読んでみましょう。そこからどのようなメッセージが読み取れるのか、ペアまたはグループで話し合ってみましょう。

- _____

- _____

- _____

- _____

- _____

- _____

>> Comprehension Check　Multiple Choice

本文の内容に照らして最も正しいものを a 〜 c の中から選んで○をつけなさい。

1. Which of the following applies to what the UN says about Reggae?

 a. Reggae is the voice only for marginalized people

 b. Reggae grew out of the Rastafarian god's prayer

 c. One of reggae's social functions is a means of praising God

2. Which of the following does NOT apply to what Laurence Cane-Honeysett says?

 a. reggae has encouraged the development of multiculturalism

 b. ska and rock steady developed from reggae

 c. reggae was very influential in Britain in the 1960s and early '70s

3. Which of the following is NOT true about followers of the Rastafarian movement?

 a. they grow marijuana for joy

 b. they have strict religious restrictions on diet

 c. some of them are/were reggae songwriters

>> English Composition for Idiom Learning　　　🔊 Audio 29

日本語の意味に合うよう、（　　　）内を並べ替えて英文を完成させましょう。並べ替え部分には本文中に登場するイディオムが含まれています。なお、文頭に来る語も小文字にしてあります。

1. 彼女は続けて説明した。

 (went, she, on, to, explain).

 ――――――――――――――――――――――――――――――

2. 彼の芸術は彼のポップカルチャー愛から生じていた。

 (grew, his, out, of, his, of, pop, art, culture, love).

 ――――――――――――――――――――――――――――――

3. 患者たちはその薬の値下げを要求している。

 (medicine, call, lower, for, prices, for, the, patients).

 ――――――――――――――――――――――――――――――

Chapter 15 | Chernobyl and the Dangerous Ground of 'Dark Tourism'

© Christopher Penler / Shutterstock.com
Virgil quote at Memorial Hall in the National 9/11 Memorial Museum.

> 旧ソ連、現ウクライナのチェルノブイリ原子力発電所事故（1984年6月発生）が起こった場所に訪れる人が引きも切らないそうだ。このような「負の遺産」に対して人はどのように向かい合うべきだろうか。

≫ Pre-reading Vocabulary Check

日本語の意味に合う英文になるよう適切なものを選びなさい。必要に応じて形を変えなさい。

> ・phenomenon　・site　・grief　・way　・morbid

1. ゆっくりやって。進むのがすごく早すぎるよ。

Slow down. You go _____ too fast.

2. 彼は病的なほどの五感の鋭さに大いに悩まされた。

He suffered much from a _____ acuteness of the senses.

3. この現象は汚染と地球温暖化によって引き起こされている。

This _____ is caused by pollution and global warming.

4. ニューメキシコのロズウェルはUFOが着陸したと思われている場所である。

Roswell, New Mexico is the supposed _____ of a UFO landing.

5. 彼の死で妻は悲しみのあまり髪が白くなってしまった。

His death grayed his wife's hair with _____.

>> Reading Passage

🔊 Audio 30

1 Chernobyl is one of the most popular examples of the phenomenon known as dark tourism – a term for visiting sites associated with death and suffering, such as Nazi concentration camps* in Europe or the 9/11 Memorial and Museum* in New York.

2 Dark tourism as a term was coined in the 1990s, by scholars exploring 5 why tourists visited sites associated with the assassination of President John F. Kennedy. The concept's also sometimes called thanatourism, – from the Greek word thanatos, meaning death, or grief tourism.

3 But visitors were traveling to sites associated with death and destruction way before the '90s. 10

4 Pompeii, the Roman city destroyed by a volcano eruption in AD79, has been on the tourist trail since the 1700s, and is still one of Italy's most-visited destinations.

© Evdoha_spb / Shutterstock.com, Archaeological ruin of ancient Roman city, Pompeii, was destroyed by Eruption of Vesuvius, volcano nearby city in Pompeii

© Curioso / Shutterstock.com, Part of Auschwitz-Birkenau Concentration Camp Holocaust Memorial Museum

5 "It's not as new as it may seem," says Peter Hohenhaus, who chronicles his experiences visiting dark tourism sites on his website, Dark-Tourism. 15 com.

6 Tony Johnston, head of Tourism at Athlone Institute of Technology in Ireland, says motivations for visiting these places vary from individual to individual, and from site to site.

7 Some visitors are there just because they're on vacation in the area, 20 others pursue a historical passion. There are also thrill seekers going for "fun," says Johnston – and a small group might have a morbid interest.

8 Most tourists behave respectfully, he clarifies.

9 "Quite often the intention of the visitor is to learn about atrocity or a

Girl in black outfit walks around the rotten floor in an abandoned sports hall in Pripyat, Ukraine, after the Chernobyl explosion.

dark heritage in a useful way, and it could be a reflection on what went wrong in the past and what lessons they can learn from the past so that mistakes aren't repeated again," says Johnston.

10 Philip Stone, executive director at the Institute for Dark Tourism Research at the UK's Lancaster University, goes as far as to say there's "no such thing as dark tourists."

11 "People who are either on vacation or on study trips [...] that doesn't make us 'dark', that just makes us interested in what's happening at these particular sites and learning from them," he says.

12 But, says Rebekah Stewart, communications and outreach manager at the Center for Responsible Travel, a Washington D.C.-based research organization, motivations do matter.

13 "Before visiting places that are associated with death and tragedy, it's important to reflect upon your intention," she tells CNN Travel. "Are you visiting to deepen your understanding and pay your respects, or are you going to check a box or take a selfie?"

NOTES

* **Nazi concentration camps**：ナチスの強制収容所
* **the 9/11 Memorial and Museum**：9.11 メモリアム・ミュージアム（ニューヨークのツインタワー跡地「グランド・ゼロ」に建てられた、2001 年 9 月 11 日に起きたアメリカ同時多発テロの追悼施設。）

≫ Post-reading Vocabulary Check

➤ 日本語の意味に合う英文になるよう、次の中から適切な 動詞 を選び、必要に応じて形を変えなさい。

・associate　・coin　・chronicle　・vary　・clarify　・deepen

1. 天候は刻々と変わった。

The weather _____ from hour to hour.

2. 微細にわたって出来事を年代順に記録したいという著者の欲求に感銘を受けている。

I'm impressed with the author's desire to _____ the events in such detail.

3. 気候変動に関連したまったく新たな問題がある。

There's a whole new problem _____ with climate change.

4. 彼女はまだ関係を深めたくなかった。

She does not want the relationship to _____ yet.

5. サイバースペースという言葉は SF 作家のウィリアム・ギブソンによって造られた。

The term cyberspace was _____ by Sci-Fi writer William Gibson.

6. この論文ではどのようにしてこのような結論が導かれたのか明らかにすることが目的である。

This paper aims to _____ how these conclusions were reached.

➤ 下記の 名詞 =英英・英日の語義が成立するように、空欄を埋めなさい。太字の名詞が空欄の場合は本文中から適切な単語を探して埋めましょう。

1. assassination = m □□□□□, political execution「暗殺」

2. concept = i □□□, notion「概念」

3. v □□□□□□ = a mountain with a hole at the top, through which hot liquid rock is forced out「火山」

4. eruption = e □□□□□□□□「噴火」

5. d □□□□□□□□□ = journey's end, landing place「目的地」

6. d □□□□□□□□□□ = the act or process of destroying something「破壊 (行為)」

7. m □□□□□□□□□ = sense of purpose, incentive「動機付け」

8. a □□□□□□□ = act of brutality, cruelty, abuse「残虐行為」

9. s □□□□□ = a photo of yourself that you take「自撮り」

≫ Comprehension Check　True or False

下の英文が本文の内容として正しい場合は T、間違っている場合は F を選びましょう。

1. The term "dark tourism" was first used when John F. Kennedy was

　　assassinated.　　　　　　　　　　　　　　　　　　　　　　(T / F)

2. Dark tourism as phenomenon first appeared in the 1990s.　　(T / F)

3. Some visit sites associated with death and suffering for fun.　(T / F)

≫ ACTIVE LEARNING for Keyword Check

本文に出てくる重要な単語についてペアまたはグループになって調べて表を完成させなさい。

用　語・テーマ	概　要
Chernobyl (The Chernobyl disaster) チェルノブイリ (チェルノブイリ原子力発電所事故)	
The assassination of John F. Kennedy ジョン・F・ケネディ大統領暗殺	
Pompeii ポンペイ火山	

>> Comprehension Check Multiple Choice

本文の内容に照らして最も正しいものを a 〜 c の中から選んで○をつけなさい。

1. Which of the following is NOT a destination of dark tourism?

　　a. Mt. Fuji

　　b. Chernobyl

　　c. Pompeii

2. Which of the following is less likely to be learned from a dark heritage site?

　　a. what caused a disaster

　　b. how we should do so that we don't make the same mistakes again

　　c. the fact that human beings enjoy death and suffering

3. Which of the following is Rebekah Stewart less likely to accept as an intention of dark tourists?

　　a. to take a selfie

　　b. to pay their respect

　　c. to deepen their understanding

>> English Composition for Idiom Learning

 Audio 31

日本語の意味に合うよう、（　　　）内を並べ替えて英文を完成させましょう。並べ替え部分には本文中に登場するイディオムが含まれています。なお、文頭に来る語も小文字にしてあります。

1. そこまでは言えないでしょう。

(I, say, wouldn't, as, far, as, to, go, that).

_____

2. 親たちは子供に対する責任をよく考えてみるべきだ。

(should, reflect, their, upon, parents, responsibilities) toward their children.

_____

3. 正解の隣の欄にチェック印をつけなさい。

(answer, next, check, the, to, the, box, right).

_____

ACKNOWLEDGEMENTS

Chapter 1: What's the Difference Between Modern and Contemporary Art?
Reprinted with permission from *Encyclopædia Britannica*, © 2019 by Encyclopædia Britannica, Inc.

Chapter 2: Jeff Koons And His Balloon Dogs
By Zuzanna Stanska. From dailyartmagzine.com, January 21, 2018. Reprinted with permission from DailyArt Magazine.com © 2018 by Zuzanna Stanska, DailyArt Magazine.

Chapter 3: The Contemporaries: Mary Sibande
By Keely Shinners. First published on artthrob.co.za, August 8, 2016 © 2016 ArtThrob, used by permission from Keely Shinners.

Chapter 4: What Languages Are Spoken In The Philippines?
By Amber Pariona. July 24, 2018 © 2018 Worldatlas.com. Used with permission of Worldatlas.com. All rights reserved.

Chapter 5: 'Latinx' explained: A history of the controversial word and how to pronounce it
By Adrianna Rodriguez. From USATODAY.com, June 29, 2019 © 2019 USA TODAY, a division of Gannett Satellite Information Network, LLC. All rights reserved. Used by permission and protected by the Copyright Laws of the United States. The printing, copying, redistribution, or retransmission of this Content without express written permission is prohibited.

Chapter 6: English Is the Language of Science. That Isn't Always a Good Thing
By Ben Panko. From smithonianmag.com, January 2, 2017 © 2017 Smithsonian Institution. Reprinted with permission from Smithsonian Enterprises. All rights reserved. Reproduction in any medium is strictly prohibited without permission from Smithsonian Institution.

Chapter 7: School Feeding Schemes Can Fill Children's Tummies and Farmers' Pockets
By Clement Mensah. From theConversation.com, March 31, 2017. Used by permission of Clement Mensah. All rights reserved.

Chapter 8: If You're Poor in America, You Can Be Both Overweight and Hungry
By Jessica Fanzo. From Bloomberg.com, July 17, 2019. Used with permission of Bloomberg L.P. Copyright © 2017. All rights reserved.

Chapter 9: This Supermarket Sells Only Wasted Food
By Erin Blakemore. From smithonianmag.com, September 27, 2016 © 2016 Smithsonian Institution. Reprinted with permission from Smithsonian Enterprises. All rights reserved. Reproduction in any medium is strictly prohibited without permission from Smithsonian Institution.

Chapter 10: The Missing Women in Workforce Data
By Aasha Kapur Mehta. From thehindubusinessline.com, January 22, 2019 © 2019 The Hindu Business Line. Reprinted with permission from Aasha Kapur Mehta and The Hindu Business Line. All rights reserved.
https://www.thehindubusinessline.com/opinion/the-missing-women-in-workforce-data/article26061484.ece

Chapter 11: Saudi Women Join the Workforce as Country Reforms
By Sarah Hassan. From CNN.com, February 7, 2018 © 2018 Cable News Network. All rights reserved. Used by permission and protected by the Copyright Laws of the United States. The printing, copying, redistribution, or retransmission of this Content without express written permission is prohibited.

Chapter 12: Migrant workers in Thailand live harsh, but improving, reality Bangkok takes legal steps to retain vital laborers from neighboring countries
By Yukako Ono, Nikkei staff writer and Akira Kodaka, Nikkei staff photographer. February 17, 2019 © Nikkei Asian Review.

Chapter 13: Chernobyl and the Dangerous Ground of 'Dark Tourism'
By Francesca Street. From CNN.com, June 25, 2019 © 2019 Cable News Network. All rights reserved. Used by permission and protected by the Copyright Laws of the United States. The printing, copying, redistribution, or retransmission of this Content without express written permission is prohibited.

Chapter 14: Reggae Officially Declared Global Cultural Treasure
By Jason Daley. From smithonianmag.com, November 30, 2018 © 2018 Smithsonian Institution. Reprinted with permission from Smithsonian Enterprises. All rights reserved. Reproduction in any medium is strictly prohibited without permission from Smithsonian Institution.

Chapter 15: A Modern History of the Ogasawara Islands: Migration, Diversity, and War
By Shun Ishihara. From Nippon.com, June 26, 2018 © 2018 the Nippon Communications Foundation. All rights reserved.
https://www.nippon.com/en/features/c05302/a-modern-history-of-the-ogasawara-islands-migration-diversity-and-war.html

The World's Big Deals: Art, Language, Food Education, Work Style and Heritage
世界を見る：アート・言語・食育・働き方改革・歴史遺産

2020 年 4 月 10 日　初版第 1 刷発行
2021 年 3 月 25 日　初版第 2 刷発行

編著者　宮本 文

発行者　森　信久
発行所　**株式会社　松柏社**
〒 102-0072　東京都千代田区飯田橋 1-6-1
TEL　03 (3230) 4813　（代表）
FAX　03 (3230) 4857
http://www.shohakusha.com
e-mail: info@shohakusha.com

英文校閲　　Howard Colefield
装　　幀　　小島トシノブ（NONdesign）
印刷・製本　日経印刷株式会社

略号 ＝ 757

ISBN978-4-88198-757-5